The Life & Legacy of

ENSLAVED VIRGINIAN

EMILY WINFREE

DR. JAN MECK AND VIRGINIA REFO

THE
History
PRESS

Published by The History Press
Charleston, SC
www.historypress.com

Back cover image, top, courtesy of Library of Congress.

First published 2021

Manufactured in the United States

ISBN 9781467150507

Library of Congress Control Number: 2021945863

Emily Winfree. *Library of Virginia.*

This book is dedicated to the thousands of families
whose stories were lost during 246 years of enslavement.

CONTENTS

CONTENTS

PREFACE

Growing up as a white child in the 1950s, I had virtually no contact with anybody who didn't look like me. I lived on an all-white street, in an all-white neighborhood, in an all-white town in the D.C. suburbs. I went to all-white schools. My lessons about race came from the now infamous fourth-grade Virginia history book. The only time I saw anybody of a different color was when we drove through D.C. to have Sunday lunch with my grandmother. I was accustomed to hearing the "n" word and other disparaging descriptions of African Americans. I knew nothing of Jim Crow laws. I had a sense that things were not right and made some feeble attempts to protest. When I was in high school, I participated in a fundraiser for an African exchange student to come to our school for a year. That resulted in my being grounded for a month. It wasn't until I went to college in Michigan that I began to learn some truths. Although sympathetic, I was a person with no understanding. I remember, in my naivete, I went to a Black Panthers meeting, all starry-eyed and wanting to help. I was called whitey and unceremoniously asked (told) to leave.

Not having any other ideas, I did what was expected of a girl of the '60s. I married, taught school, divorced (that was not expected), became a single parent and concentrated on my career at NASA for twenty-nine years, a bystander in the struggle. After I retired, I became a docent at the Virginia Historical Society (now the Virginia Museum of History and Culture, VMHC). As I learned the content of its "Story of Virginia" gallery, I became more and more outraged at the lies I had been told in school and

Emily Winfree's cottage, sitting on rails next to the notorious Lumpkin's Jail site in Shockoe Bottom. *Authors' photograph.*

by my parents. It became my passion to learn as much as I could about the true history of African Americans in my town of Richmond, Virginia. It is probably the best place in the country to do so, having been the capital of the Confederacy and a major purveyor of human beings. I started doing oral histories of elderly African Americans. I read everything I could get my hands on. I enrolled in "tour guide school." As I learned more, I designed a tour called "African American Heroes of Richmond" and started giving it for free to anybody who would go with me. I gave it to the new president and CEO of the VMHC, Jamie Bosket.

On one particular Sunday, I had convinced a group of mostly elderly women from a local African American church to take my tour. Many were reluctant. They didn't know why a white woman was doing this, and they didn't want to hear the same depressing stories of brutality and privation. But they came, I guess to be polite. As we drove around town, I told stories of heroic people like James Lafayette, Madison Washington, Gabriel and Henry "Box" Brown, and I could see their spirits lifting. I remember, we were down in Shockoe Bottom and I was talking about Gabriel's failed insurrection.

I pointed up to the overpass on Broad Street and said, "That's where the historical marker about him stands. He was hanged on gallows right below it." Before I could get the next sentence out of my mouth, there they went, on their walkers, making their way across the field, up the concrete stairs and across the busy street to see that marker. When they returned, some had tears in their eyes, took my hands and thanked me for telling these stories. That was the moment I finally started to understand. They live in a city cluttered with Confederate monuments and statues; where African American cemeteries are choked with weeds; where their communities (and even some of the ladies' homes) were torn down to make way for highways and coliseums and replaced with housing projects. We were standing on the very spot where their ancestors were imprisoned, tortured and sold. Yet their stories have been invisible.

Right beside us, sitting on a trailer, was a little run-down clapboard cottage, formerly owned by an African American woman. It is now owned by the city and had been sitting there, abandoned, for nineteen years. It represented yet another untold story about African Americans in Richmond. That was when I decided to research the story of that clapboard cottage and its owner, Emily Winfree, and make it known to the people of Richmond. I asked for the help of my friend Virginia Refo, an experienced genealogist, and together we worked for three years researching Mrs. Winfree. The result is this book. One hundred percent of the royalties will go to the new Emily Winfree Education Fund at the VMHC, which also now sponsors my tour. Our hope is that the final result of these efforts will be that the cottage is restored and made into an educational venue for the African American history of Richmond, Virginia.

—Jan Meck

ACKNOWLEDGEMENTS

*I*t truly took a village to bring this story to light. The difficulties of dealing with old documents, old legalese and forgotten stories were overcome with the help of so many. Foremost was the help of Emily Winfree's family. The recollections of Emily Grace Jones Jefferson, Emily Winfree's great-granddaughter, brought the entire story of Emily's children and grandchildren to life. The abundance of old photographs provided by Robert Goins Jr., Emily's great-great-grandson, put faces to those who are gone. He even welcomed me into his home to go through old photo albums and choose the best ones to scan and use. Sylvia Wilson Richie, Emily's great-great-granddaughter, and Charles Hicks Sr., great-grandson, also provided photos and family stories for the book. Emily Jones McGowan, Emily's great-great-granddaughter, offered important details about her father's stellar musical career.

As soon as people heard what we were trying to do, they enthusiastically jumped in to help. When we ran into problems getting clear images of 150-year-old documents, Jill Balsalmo at the Chesterfield County Courthouse, Danicia Patrice Boone at the Petersburg Courthouse and Andrew Foster at the Virginia Museum of History and Culture all went out of their way to get usable copies for us. When we were confused by 150-year-old legal documents, John R. Pagan, professor emeritus at the University of Richmond, stepped up to help.

And all along the way, the wonderful staff and volunteers at the Chesterfield County Historical Society, Magnolia Grange, the Virginia Museum of

History and Culture and the Library of Virginia were incredibly helpful. Minor Weisiger allowed us to use his father's research on the Pattesons.

Most special thanks must be given to Melvin Hawkins, Ed Willeman, Marie Barnett and Paul Little of Manchester Lodge #14. They helped us find an original record of money paid to Emily Winfree for her services as a cook at their lodge. They also went to extraordinary efforts to find a missing picture of Emily, even to the extent of drilling open their safe. Sadly, the original picture was never found. And of course, Jamie Bosket, president and CEO of the Virginia Museum of History and Culture, who put the resources of the VMHC at our disposal and hosted a reunion for the family, must be thanked.

There are also people who helped with the technical details of putting this together. Our editor, Kate Jenkins, was the first to see the potential in this book, and she was instrumental in making it the best it could be. My husband, Del Kayser, provided much-needed technical expertise and assistance, and he read this manuscript and provided feedback an untold number of times.

INTRODUCTION

*T*he names and accomplishments of some Virginians roll off our tongues like water. More than nine hundred books have been written about our first president, who left a profound legacy in Virginia and our nation. But the stories of lesser-known Virginians are important as well. There are many who never knew fame or acquired fortunes yet persevered against overwhelming odds. They also left legacies. Emily Winfree is one such woman. Her descendants, who have been able to prosper because of her strength and tenacity, are her legacy. Mrs. Winfree, an African American woman who lived through slavery, the Civil War, Reconstruction and Jim Crow, never surrendered to the appalling circumstances that surrounded her; she never stopped trying to make a better life for her children. No matter the challenge, she kept her family together and, through them and their descendants, ultimately prevailed.

Our quest to learn as much as we could about Emily Winfree began when we first saw a dilapidated little clapboard structure sitting on a trailer down in a flood zone called Shockoe Bottom in Richmond, Virginia. The Bottom is named after Shockoe Creek, which used to run through there, but now is covered over and part of the sewer system. Shockoe is derived from Shacahocan, a Powhatan/Algonquin name. This low-lying area was where the antebellum tobacco warehouses were and where many free and enslaved African American industrial workers lived. It was also the center of the Richmond slave trade, including one of the most notorious slave jails, Lumpkin's Jail. After the Civil War, Shockoe Bottom became an industrial/business area for many years. Now, the area where the cottage sits is primarily paved over as a parking lot for Virginia Commonwealth University. The cottage was not originally situated where it currently resides. When Emily Winfree lived in it with her children, it was across the James River in Manchester. In 2002, its address was 209 Commerce Avenue, and it was about to be torn down by Taylor and Parish Construction, which wanted to expand its parking lot. A group of dedicated volunteers, the Alliance to Conserve Old Richmond Neighborhoods (ACORN), persuaded Expert House Movers to move the cottage to the city-owned property behind the Exxon station on Broad Street. ACORN tried to work with the City of Richmond to develop a plan to restore the cottage and find a permanent home for it. They began raising money for the restoration, but a folder full of paperwork tracks the problems that occurred within the city's bureaucracy, and in the end, nothing came of the effort, and the money was returned to the donors. Although restoration of the cottage has been almost constantly discussed, it sits still on the trailer. The year is now 2021. The cottage has gained some publicity, and various articles have appeared in local publications, but no systematic effort has been made to really learn about Emily Winfree and how she related to this cottage. We set out on a quest for original documents and materials, and after many months of searching, we are now able to chronicle the life of Emily Winfree and six generations of her family, and we have proven that the cottage was given to her by her former owner and the father of some of her children, David Winfree. What we learned about this woman and her family is truly inspirational.

We have given presentations about Emily Winfree and her cottage to organizations around Richmond but decided it was necessary to write this book. That decision derived from two goals. The first was to honor this remarkable woman who survived so much and prevailed through so much hardship. The second was to raise awareness that it is critically important to Richmond's healing that her cottage be restored. Here, then, is the story. The authors have taken the liberty of adding imagined conversations and scenarios to the factual data in hopes of enhancing the immersion of the reader into the lives of Emily and her family.

Chapter 1

SIX CURIOUS CHILDREN

All six children were scrambling for the best position. "Get off my foot. You're squishing me," squeaked Emily Grace, the youngest. Though petite, she was fearless and scrappy, always right in the thick of things. Stephen scraped her off the floor and plopped her on his shoulders. "Stop squirming or you'll fall." "Shhh, if you all don't shut up and be still, nobody will hear anything," whispered Walter. Mae immediately declared, "You said shut up! I'm telling Mama! You're gonna get it." All this wrangling arose from their determination to hear what the adults were saying on the other side of that thick oaken door. Walter's warning was prophetic, shut up notwithstanding. Without warning, the door flew open and all six children went tumbling into the room, landing in a noisy, tangled knot of arms and legs, the adults glaring at them. "What on God's green earth are you children doing?" scolded their mother. "We have told you and told you; when we close that door, we are discussing a topic that is not for the ears of children, especially such disobedient ones. Now, I believe you all have chores to do, and I'm betting you haven't finished them. So get to it." As usual, the inquisitive Jones children had been foiled. It was useless to argue, because Mama's word was law. Dejected, they trudged away to their chores as Grandma "Moosh" watched in silence. She never liked to see her babies in trouble.

"What could be the big secret?" wondered Cornelia. "We know they were only talking about Great-grandma Emily and Great-grandpa David, but they passed away ages ago. What secret would matter after all this time?" "I don't know, but one day I'll figure out how to listen in," said Stephen. Little did the children know that when the secrets about Emily and David were finally revealed to them, four-year-old Emily Grace would be the only one of the six siblings who had not gone to heaven. These six children were Stephen, Mary Lydia (Mae), Cornelia, John Robert, Walter Douglas Jr. and Emily Grace Jones. We shall hear more about them later.

*T*his scene might have unfolded in the home of Mr. and Mrs. Jones (Walter Douglas Jones and Mary Elizabeth Walker Jones), an African American family who lived at 814 West Marshall Street in Richmond, Virginia, in the prosperous African American community of Jackson Ward. Their street was named for John Marshall, the famous chief justice of the United States Supreme Court, whose house (which had become a museum) was just a few blocks away. Jackson Ward was a gerrymandered district that was created in 1871 to concentrate the majority of African American voters in Richmond into one voting district. Although handicapped by Jim Crow laws and policies, prominent leaders such as entrepreneur Maggie Walker, newspaper editor John Mitchell, architect Charles Russell and others helped Jackson Ward become one of the most important African American residential and business districts in the nation. It was a thriving, self-sufficient community that was called the "Harlem of the South" and the "Black Wall Street." Jackson Ward had its own African American–owned banks, architects, physicians, dentists, lawyers, shops, churches, insurance companies, restaurants, funeral homes, pharmacies, retail stores and entertainment venues. The Hippodrome Theater, opened in 1914, was known nationwide, and such luminaries as Billie Holiday, Ella Fitzgerald, Nat King Cole, Ray Charles, Louis Armstrong and Duke Ellington performed there. Jackson Ward was also a center of the jazz scene. One local group, Roy Johnson's Happy Pals, became nationally famous. They played at the Savoy Ballroom in New York and once beat out Duke Ellington in a jazz contest in New York City. Residents could find plenty of wholesome entertainment every Saturday night on Second Street, known as the Deuce.

Tragically, in the 1950s, the white establishment cut Jackson Ward in half by routing construction of I-95 right through it and later destroyed the eastern part to build the Richmond Coliseum and expand the Medical College of Virginia. The residents were moved out of Jackson Ward. Public housing projects were built. Emily Winfree's great-granddaughter told us of how she went to her old house to try to rescue family papers before the house was torn down. Today, Jackson Ward is a shell of its former self, but when the previous scene occurred, it was thriving.

The Jones family was respected in the community, active in civic affairs and leaders in Ebenezer Baptist Church. Mr. Jones was the grandson of the founder of the church. He was a mechanic (trained at Hampton Institute) and had a shop in the backyard. Mrs. Jones was a teacher in Richmond. The family was close. Growing up in Jim Crow Richmond, they had to be.

The shoe store of St. James Gilpin on Broad Street in Richmond, circa 1899. His daughter Zenobia Gilpin became a prominent physician in Richmond. *Library of Congress.*

Prosperous Thompson and Benson Pharmacy on Leigh Street in Jackson Ward, circa 1899. *Library of Congress.*

Young men learning to assemble telephones at Hampton Institute, formerly Hampton Normal, now Hampton University. *Library of Congress.*

Young women in cooking class at Hampton Institute. *Library of Congress.*

Also, with only two and a half bedrooms and one bath, closeness was a given—privacy a hopeless fantasy. The year was about 1930; Emily Grace was four.

Grandma "Moosh," Mrs. Jones's mother, lived with them. Her name was really Maria (pronounced with a long *i*) Winfree Walker, but Emily Grace called her Moosh, so Grandma Moosh she was, much beloved by all six children. She was their constant companion while the parents worked, as well as their direct link to their great-grandparents. The Jones children frequently tried to pry information about David, their mysterious great-grandfather, from her. Once in a while, they would get a little tidbit. They were told that he was very fond of their great-grandmother Emily. They heard that he had bought her a house and a farm, but they weren't sure if that was true. I asked Emily Grace if she knew if David and Emily had ever married, and she told me that was what was being discussed when they got sent out of the room. What they did not know was that their great-grandfather had owned their great-grandmother and their beloved grandmother. Maybe they also didn't know he was white.

So who was Maria Winfree Walker, Grandma Moosh? Let us introduce you.

Chapter 2

MARIA WINFREE WALKER

A CHILD IS BORN

In her cramped, stuffy quarters in the attic of the big house, eighteen-year-old Emily's labor pains had grown to a crescendo. The contractions had started off easy, but now, after six hours, they were agonizing. She was trying to muffle her sobs with the sheet so as to not make too much noise in her pain. Her mother was at her side. The midwife had orchestrated everything: hot water, towels, scissors, string—everything was at the ready. After nine long months, and just after midnight, a new baby girl made her appearance. Her skin was much lighter than her mother's, but this didn't surprise anyone in the room. Wailing as she confronted the world in which her life would unfold, the baby was no longer protected in the warm, safe womb of her mother. She seemed to intuit that she had emerged into a harsh environment. As Emily took her in her arms, the wonderment of a mother's love for her child was overshadowed by the stark reality of their situation. For Emily had no husband—could have no husband. She had no legal right to her child, who, on the instant of her birth, was enslaved by the same man who enslaved Emily and her whole family. Her baby could be taken from her at that moment or at any moment henceforth. Her daughter could not marry; would not be educated; could be beaten, raped, sold and even murdered with impunity. Still, Emily was resolved. She made a vow to do anything, sacrifice anything to protect her. She named her daughter Maria. The year was 1856.

"Grandma Moosh"

We had the privilege of hearing about that baby girl, Grandma Moosh, 162 years later from her granddaughter Emily Grace Jones Jefferson, who shared with us her recollections of her beloved grandmother. You see, Emily Grace was the youngest of the six Jones children. Theirs was a very busy and crowded household. Both parents worked very hard to keep food on the table. At times, when other family members had troubles, they would come live with the family as well. Being the smallest, Emily sometimes got lost in the shuffle, but her grandmother was her refuge. She always took the extra time with her. Emily Grace's earliest memory was falling off to sleep at night, safely nestled in her grandmother's warm lap and enfolded in her arms. There they were, in the quiet of the slumbering house, gently rocking until the child was fast asleep and still there when the sun welcomed the next morning. "I would fall asleep in her arms, and in the morning I would still be there. She would have sat up all night so I could sleep." When she was a little older, Emily Grace slept in the bed with Grandma Moosh. When I asked Emily Grace how to spell Moosh, she said, "I don't know. I had a lisp as a child, and that was how I said her name. Everybody else tried to cure me of the lisp, but Grandma Moosh just told me not to worry because I would grow out of it." She admits that her grandma spoiled her terribly. Although discipline was strict in the Jones household, it was different for Emily Grace. Moosh told her she would never let her be whipped because her name was Emily, after Moosh's beloved mother.

Maria sometimes told the Jones children stories about her mother, like how she was the cook at the Possum Lodge. The children laughed because that was such a silly name. She told them it was called the Possum Lodge because, after the war, times were so hard that they couldn't afford a turkey for Thanksgiving, so they had to cook possums. She told them a little about their great-grandfather too. Maria was ten when he died, so she would have remembered him. She remembered he was very fond of her mother. She knew they had a little house, and she thought he had bought it for them, but she wasn't sure if that was true. When I informed Emily Grace that it was indeed true because we had found the deed to that house, she was surprised and pleased. The one thing Moosh wouldn't talk about was the marital status of their great-grandparents. That was always when they were sent from the room.

Emily Grace recounted scenes when their grandma took the children about town on the streetcar. "She was very light, as white as a piece of paper." This led to some amusement for them on the streetcar. The car ran down Marshall Street and stopped right in front of their house "because the conductor would hear about it if it didn't. The conductor would step down and help grandma aboard, and she would take a seat in the front, in the 'whites only' section." Then the six children (who were all darker-skinned) would board, file on to the back of the car and take their seats in the "colored section." When they arrived at their stop, the conductor would assist their grandmother off the car. She would then turn and call out, "Come along, grandchildren," and they would all come from the back and follow after her. Emily Grace chuckled as she described the white folks with their mouths hanging open in amazement at this white woman with all the little "colored" children." They were accustomed to seeing an African American "nanny" escorting white children, not the other way around. The children would then follow Moosh on down the street, attending to whatever business they were about.

Grandma Moosh always wore a white blouse and black skirt; in fact, she wore five skirts, all with pockets. Emily Grace was small enough that she could hide beneath the skirts if she needed to feel safe. "She would always carry candy for us in the pocket of one skirt and cookies in another. The pocket of the innermost skirt was where she kept her money. She didn't trust banks." When I asked Emily where her grandmother got her money, she said that her other grown children would send it to her. One of Maria's sons lived in California, and several times he sent her travel money so she could go visit him. Sometimes money for Maria would arrive in the mail in two envelopes, one inside the other. On the outer envelope was the address and postage. On the inner envelope was written, "Don't take your grandmother's money." Although Maria did not trust banks, Emily Grace had a little savings account in Mrs. Maggie Walker's Penny Savings Bank. She remembers seeing Mrs. Walker out and about on the streets of Jackson Ward.

Maria was very dignified and proper and constantly corrected the children's English. However, on occasion she was heard to use some very colorful, or rather off-color, language, and when that happened, she told the children not to tell their mother. She is known to have said "bitch" from time to time. Although wise in the ways of the world, Maria never learned to read or write, and she well knew the disadvantages that accompanied her lack of learning. She ingrained in the children the importance of an education and insisted that they all excel in school. All six of them attended college and had successful careers. Actually, truth be told, Emily Grace says that the real reason she wanted to become educated was so that she could earn enough money to buy a house with more than one bathroom; in this, she succeeded. She graduated from Virginia Union University and later became a librarian in the Library of Congress in Washington, D.C. Another motivation for Emily Grace to do well in school was to be able to assist her grandmother. Maria would often hand her a book and ask her to read it to her or ask her to read her mail to her. She also dictated her letters to young Emily, who would dutifully write them out and address the envelopes for her.

The Jones family was close, and that was important for survival in those times. Emily Grace told us how difficult and even dangerous life was for African Americans in Jim Crow Richmond. She said that the girls could not walk down Broad Street unless one of their brothers was with them because white men would accuse them of being prostitutes. This was very dangerous, as rape of black women was a big problem. "But if you worked for a white family and had on a uniform, that would protect you." However, working as a domestic servant in a white household was also dangerous for African American girls. It was common knowledge that many of them were violated by the white men in the house, and many fathers would not allow their daughters to take such employment. That is one reason why the Jones family insisted their children get a good education.

Another painful memory was that of shopping. In white-owned department stores, African Americans were sometimes not allowed in the front door; not allowed to try on or return clothing; or required to step aside when a white person came up and wait to be served until all the white customers had been helped. Maggie Walker opened a department store so that people could shop with dignity, but white store owners manipulated her suppliers to stop selling to her, and that forced the store to close.

There is not room here to expound upon all the injustices served up to the African American community. These are only a few inflicted on them during Jim Crow, but they were marked in the mind and worldview of the young girl who still talks about them all these years later. No amount of success in life can erase them. Today, Emily Grace laments the fact that younger generations don't understand what it was like in Richmond back then. Younger family members often ask her why she would let people talk to her and treat her the way they did. She tells them, "Because I'd be dead if I didn't." Those were dangerous times. Many lynchings occurred in Virginia, although not as many as in the Deep South states. In 2015, the Equal Justice Initiative of Montgomery, Alabama, counted seventy-six lynchings in Virginia between 1877 and 1950. Emily Grace grew up knowing of the terror around her.

But Grandma Moosh protected her grandchildren from anybody, no matter who it was. "She wasn't afraid of anything." She would stride down to the courthouse on Marshall Street, children in tow, and talk to the white judges. They all knew and respected her and would come down off the bench to converse with her, while Emily Grace listened intently, hidden beneath Moosh's skirts. Sometimes Maria and a judge would engage in general conversation, but her real purpose was to make sure the judges knew all of her grandchildren. She told the judges that her grandchildren were all good children. She told them that if there was ever an incident involving any of her grandchildren, the police were to first call her, and she would come down and take care of it. And that's just what happened on the rare times there was trouble. This continued even after the children were grown and working. She also would go down and inform the judges when anything untoward happened in the neighborhood and let them know that she expected them to take care of it. She was representing and protecting the children of the entire neighborhood. "As bad as segregation was, it helped us to love each other and take care of each other and that was the good that came of it. Most families were large, the neighborhood was close and the children were always in and out of each other's houses. A mother might call our house and say, 'If you see my boy at your house, send him on home.'" All that was before Jackson Ward was destroyed by the highway and many of the families were sent to live in the projects.

Emily Grace was ten years old when Maria died. She still gets choked up when she speaks of her. She had lost the person who probably had the greatest influence on her, and whom she loved dearly, and it was very hard for her. But the gifts that her Grandma Moosh gave her have lasted a lifetime.

So how did the baby girl, born into slavery in 1856, end up living at 814 West Marshall Street in Richmond? To answer that question, we must tell you the story of her mother, the great-grandmother of the six curious Jones children, Emily Winfree.

Chapter 3

EMILY WINFREE

*I*n the earliest record we found of Emily, she was enslaved in the household of Jordan Branch, a lawyer and the powerful sheriff of Petersburg, Virginia. The year was 1857. It is possible that she grew up in that house. She lived there along with her "mother," MaryAnn (Stokes), and MaryAnn's other children, Agnes, Reuben, Sam and Lizzie. We cannot say with certainty that MaryAnn actually was Emily's mother, as there are no documents and we have found nothing about Emily's birth. The most frustrating part of this kind of research is that it is so very difficult to find records, even last names, of those who were enslaved over the course of two centuries. We have explored every possible avenue in our attempts to find a definitive document about Emily's parents, with no luck. There are hints, though, here and there, from which we can speculate. We found three different surnames for Emily on different official documents. On her own death certificate, which was informed by her son Clifford, Emily's parents are listed as John W. Scott and Emily Jones. Clifford was a schoolteacher, so he had some education. One might trust his knowledge of his mother's birth except for the fact that he was misinformed about his own father's name. On the death certificate of Emily's daughter Lucy, Emily's maiden name is Jones. On her son Henry's death certificate, Emily's maiden name is Stokes. Of the three names, we do have evidence that Emily kept in touch with the Stokes family long after the war, although that doesn't necessarily mean they were family. So, in the end, we don't know who Emily's parents were.

The home of Jordan Branch in Petersburg, where Emily and Maria were enslaved, as it looks today. *Authors' photograph.*

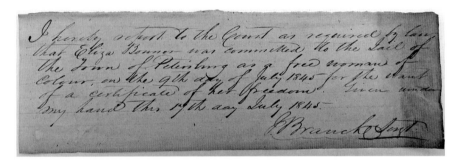

Above: The report signed by Jordan Branch of his arrest of the free woman Eliza Bonner for want of certification of her freedom, 1845. *Library of Virginia.*

Left: On the back of the previous image, Eliza Bonner is ordered to be hired out for a period not exceeding twelve months, 1845. *Library of Virginia.*

Back to our story. The Branch family was prominent and powerful in Petersburg and firmly embedded in the slavocracy. Jordan's older brother Thomas owned Branch and Son, a firm that held auctions to sell and hire out enslaved people and brokered bond agreements between owners and hirers. Jordan himself owned many people. As sheriff, he routinely arrested and jailed people who had tried to escape enslavement, as well as free African Americans who were without their registers of freedom. He would instruct jailers to hold these people until they proved their free status *and* paid any jail fees accrued. The *and* is the key word, for even if they proved their free status, if they were unable to pay the jailers' fees, the law required they would be "hired out." This was only one of the many dangers to, and restrictions on, free Black people.

THE PERILS OF FREEDOM

Given the horrors of slavery, the average person might naturally assume that every enslaved person would do anything to obtain his or her freedom. But there were so many obstacles that prevented escape. An enslaved person could run but would have to make it to a free state that allowed "colored" people. After the Fugitive Slave Law was passed in 1850, escapees would have to get all the way to Canada to be safe. For a person who had lived in bondage, with no education or knowledge of the outside world, it was a forbidding journey through swamps and forests and unmarked trails with torn clothing and nothing to eat. It meant leaving loved ones behind, not knowing when, if ever, they would meet again. It meant the ever-present danger of recapture. Those who were apprehended were often beaten, tortured, mutilated or even murdered with impunity.

In 1838, George B. Ripley, Esq., from Norwich, Connecticut, furnished a statement in a letter dated December 12. It involved a discussion between a planter in Nansemond County (now part of the city of Suffolk), Virginia, and Gurdon Chapman, Esq., who was buying a cargo of corn from the planter. The planter described his treatment of runaways thus:

> *I'll tell you how I treat my runaway n-----s. I had a big n----- that ran away the second time; as soon as I got track of him I took three good fellows and went in pursuit, and found him in the night, some miles distant, in a corn house; we took him and ironed him hand and foot, and carted him home.*

The next morning we tied him to a tree, and whipped him until there was not a sound place on his back. I then tied his ankles and hoisted him up to a limb—feet up and head down—we then whipped him until the damned n----- smoked so that I thought he would take fire and burn up. We then took him down; and to make sure that he would not run away the third time, I run my knife in back of the ankles and cut off the large cords—and then I ought to have put some lead into the wounds, but I forgot it." Mr. Ripley states that "The truth of the above is of unquestionable authority; and you may publish or suppress it, as shall best subserve the cause of God and humanity."[1]

One might assume that a free African American in Virginia had rights and privileges similar to those of white people. Nothing was further from the truth. The lives of "free negroes" were fraught with danger and difficulty. John Russel's book *The Free Negro in Virginia, 1619–1865*, paints a clear picture of the situation.[2] Whites feared that "free negroes" would cause unrest and insurrection in the enslaved population, so every attempt was made to keep their numbers at a minimum. Virginia laws against them became more and more restrictive, with the goal of minimizing their numbers and controlling their lives. After May 1, 1806, manumitted slaves were required to leave Virginia within a year. But where were they to go? By 1807, Maryland, Kentucky and Delaware had passed laws forbidding freedmen to take up residence in their states, and during the next twenty-five years, Ohio, Indiana, Illinois, Missouri, North Carolina and Tennessee followed suit. Even Oregon, far out west, prohibited "colored" people from entering when it became a territory. Imagine the situation in which one member of an enslaved family had gained his freedom, but the rest had not. That person would have to leave, perhaps never seeing family members again. Should he go and try to earn money to buy the rest of the family? Should he stay enslaved, hoping to keep the family together but risking separation by sale? These were the kind of inhumane laws that were imposed on these people. During our research on Emily, we discovered, in an archived folder at the Library of Virginia, dozens of petitions to the Virginia General Assembly from the year 1806. They were all from freed people begging permission to be allowed to stay in Virginia.

In another attempt to remove freed people, the American Colonization Society was founded in 1816 to start a colony in Africa to which they might be sent. This became the focus of "solving the free negro problem" for the next twenty-five years. Most attempts at colonization failed. So many people were just plain stuck.

A list of six free persons committed to jail in Petersburg for the want of register by the mayor of said city, 1856. *Library of Virginia.*

A most insidious threat to free people of color in Virginia came in 1813, when a special poll (head) tax of $1.50 was imposed on all male African Americans older than sixteen. In 1815, it was raised to $2.50 and applied to ages sixteen through forty-five. The tax was dropped in 1816 but reinstated in 1850 at the rate of $1.00 on men between the ages of twenty-one and fifty-five. The revenues were to have been used for colonization efforts, but most of the monies went into the general treasury.[3] Those who could not pay the tax were jailed.

In addition to the poll tax, people were required to pay an additional $0.25 for a copy of the register (receipt) and keep that with them at all times, available to show to any authority figure who might stop them. These were their "free papers." Woe unto any free African American man or woman found to be without their papers. They were held in jail for periods of up to several months because of "want of register." As they waited in jail, they accumulated hefty jailer's fees. Records from the Richmond City Jail Register document the story of Lucy Briggs, a free Negro woman who, on November 22, 1841, was found at large in the city of Richmond and arrested for "want of her free papers." She remained in jail until April 25, 1842, when she finally proved her free status in court.[4] However, since she could not pay the $59.38 jail "support" debt she had accumulated while in jail, she was hired out at public auction at the "Old Market" to one Benjamin Wropper (who paid her debt) for a period of fifty-nine years. We do not know why Briggs did not have her papers. Had she lost them? Could she not afford the $0.25 to get a copy? Did she absentmindedly leave them behind while running an errand? The danger of making one little mistake like this was part of the endless series of traps by which free people could be ensnared.[5]

The following quotations from the *Daily Dispatch* in Richmond illustrate the result of people not having papers with them. It is worth pointing out that in all three cases, the prisoners were known to be free women but were arrested anyway.

> *September 11, 1856: Committed: Elizabeth Johnson, a free girl, was committed to prison for want of a register.*
> *December 2, 1856: Committed: Sarah Green, a free negress, was sent to prison by the Mayor, for want of a register of her freedom.*
> *February 21, 1856: No papers: Louisa Jenkins, a free girl, was committed to jail, by order of the recorder, for want of a register of her freedom.*

On February 3, 1853, the *Daily Dispatch* ran this ad:

> *Lost on Saturday last, between Valley St. and Rockett's, a leather pocket book containing my free papers and three dollars and sixty-eight cents. The finder can have the money by returning my free papers to me, or leaving them at this office. HENRY SCOTT a free man of color.*

It is just one of many ads for lost papers we found in the newspapers. We wonder if Mr. Scott's papers were restored to him.

The slave markets in Richmond were second only to those in New Orleans at that time, and demand was high on the plantations in the Deep South.[6] One can assume that corruption was rampant in such a system, with people being arrested so they would end up in the slave market when demand for labor was high. A similar process was used later in the Jim Crow South. African American men were arrested on bogus charges and charged court costs, which were then paid by local whites in exchange for forced labor, sometimes for life.

Restrictions on free African Americans were seemingly endless. They could not vote or hold office, testify in the trial of a white person or have a trial by jury. They were restricted in their right to own firearms, which put a burden on farmers who needed to protect their crops and livestock.

They were required to provide service to the military. As of 1832, they could not own a person who wasn't their own spouse or child (later on, parents were also included). Enslaved family members were often bought by their free family members so they would be protected from the slave markets or banishment. However, if the "owner" died without furnishing the proper paperwork to free his family, the family was deemed by the state to be "slaves without owners" and became the property of the state and could be sold. In one such case, Sally Dabney was purchased by her husband in 1818. When he died, his will bequeathed all his possessions to her but failed to explicitly state that she was to be freed. As a slave, she was legally not competent to inherit, and all his property went to the "Literary Fund" (established in 1810 to support public education). Her status being unresolved, she was forced to petition the General Assembly and bring forth witnesses as to her husband's intent to free her before the state finally passed a special act recognizing her freedom.[7] These kinds of perils faced free people at every turn, and there was a constant stream of petitions to the state asking to be excused from one restriction or another.

The above discussion makes it clear that freedom was obviously not the panacea for African Americans that some may assume.

But let us return to Emily and Maria.

EMILY AND MARIA ARE SOLD

Jordan Branch died intestate in September 1857. In order to settle the estate, the law required an inventory and appraisal of his estate. Emily and Maria were appraised, along with the furniture and dining room china. Emily is listed as twenty years old, child of MaryAnn, with a child, Maria. Their combined appraised value was $800. Records conflict regarding Emily's true age. Her gravestone reflects a birth year of 1834. Her death certificate clearly states her age as seventy-seven on January 10, 1919, which would give her a birth year of 1842. If she was twenty in 1857, she would have been born in 1837. So she bore Maria sometime between the ages of thirteen and nineteen. Fourteen was the age at which an enslaved girl was considered ready to start having children. However, any professional appraiser probably would not mistake a thirteen-year-old for a twenty-year-old, making us believe that 1834 or 1837 is most likely to be the correct birth year.

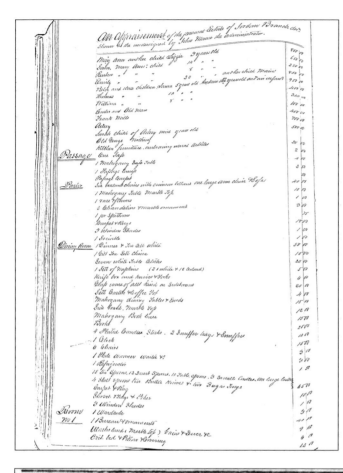

Left: Appraisement of the personal estate of Jordan Branch, dec.d. Emily and daughter Maria are appraised at $800, 1857. *Petersburg Hustings Court Will Book #4.*

Below: *Daily Dispatch*, December 27, 1858, advertisement for sale of the Branch estate, including Emily and Maria, on the next day. *Library of Congress.*

ADMINISTRATOR'S SALE OF 23 VALUABLE NEGROES AT PUBLIC AUCTION. I shall, on TUESDAY, the 28th day of December, 1858, in front of Branch & Son's store, on Old street, Petersburg, Va, sell at public auction, 23 Negroes, belonging to the estate of the late Jordan Branch, embracing house servants, cook, washer and ironer, seamstress, factory hands, laborers, boys and girls. These are family servants and are sold for no fault, but to settle up the estate. Terms cash.
JOHN MANN, Adm'r.
BRANCH & SON, Aucts.   de 14—tds

All the Branch inventory was sold at auction on December 28, 1858. An ad was run in the *Daily Dispatch* the day before the sale. The ad states that the "valuable negroes" were being sold through no fault of their own. This praise notwithstanding, up on the block they went.

The Night Before the Auction
MaryAnn

Oh my poor sweet child! How can I stand to lose her now? Ever since she was a baby she has been by my side. She came right after Agnes. How I had Agnes in the first place was a very brutal thing that happened to me. They sent that big carpenter over from Old Man Winfree's to work on the new buttery, and he just wouldn't keep off me. Lord, I tried everything I could to keep out of his way, but he was working in the house and I was the cook, so there I was, and finally one night he got me. I was only fourteen and didn't know what was happening; I just knew that it hurt something awful, and then he was off me and gone. There wasn't a thing I could do about it or anybody I could tell, because that's just the way things are in this world. My mama and papa were gone, but they couldn't have protected me anyway. He was hanging around here for about a week after that, but then he finished the buttery and went back where he came from, and I never saw him again. I was so scared the whole time I carried her, and afraid I would hate her, but as soon as she was born I fell in love with her the minute I laid these eyes on her. I've had three more children since then, but it was with somebody I cared about.

I sure enough know how hard it is to lose your family. When I was ten years old, Master James died, and my mama and papa were sold away from that farm in Lynchburg, and Master Jordan, he needed a cook's helper, so I ended up here. I cried myself to sleep every night for a long time but finally gave up and just did my cooking. I do the best I can, and I never have been whipped here like we were before, so I thank the Lord for that. And I'm the head cook now, so that means extra rations for my children. They're lucky; none of them have to go out at dawn to work in the fields. They all have inside jobs. Agnes is one of the best housekeepers in Petersburg and seems to always have a cheerful face. Sam, he's real smart, so they use him down at the store. He's even learned to cipher. He's getting too smart for his britches though. He's all the time talking about running, but I told him to just forget about that. Get it out of his mind. He'd be caught for sure, and I've seen those boys when they bring them back, all tore up and bloody after the slave catchers got through with them. He don't have much chance of getting away anyhow, but if he did, I would never see him again. I told him the best thing for him would be to get real good at ciphering and maybe they would let him keep some of his pay and one day he could buy himself outta here.

But my Emily never caused any trouble. She grew up by my side and learned to be a real good cook. Same thing happened to her that happened to me though, and that's how we got our baby Maria. She won't tell me who got at her. I think it could be Master Jordan's son

David. He and Emily grew up together in this house. When they were little kids, they were always playing together under the kitchen table while I worked, laughing and trying to steal cookies and cake. You couldn't hardly get them apart until David was about thirteen, and then he started ordering Emily around and saying she had to call him Mister David and do everything he told her without asking why. They weren't so close after that, but lots of times I saw him looking at her kind of funny, and next thing I know, there's Maria. Of course, it could be Master Jordan's brother-in-law Dr. Winfree. He's all the time over here visiting his nephews, and he had plenty of chances to be with Emily too. And we heard that he's sending an agent tomorrow to buy her and Maria for himself. But it doesn't really matter who Maria's father is cause, like I said, that's just the way it is. From what I've seen of him, Dr. David is not a cruel man, so maybe it will be OK if he gets her. She's a real good cook now, and I told her just don't do nothing to make him mad. So I told her always keep your head down and don't look directly at him and it will be all right. If he does buy them, they won't be so far away and maybe she can get a pass to visit sometimes.

Emily

It's almost dawn, so this is the day. Lord, it's freezing cold in this room. I know it's below zero out there, and the auction will be outside. I wonder if they'll make me stand up on the block. Here's my poor baby, sound asleep. I love to hear her soft snoring. She has no idea that today her world will be turned upside down. She won't understand why she can't see Grandma anymore. Or Sam and Reuben, who always teases her and makes her laugh. And little Lizzie. How can I tell her that she won't have her little aunt and best friend to play with? This same thing happened to Mama when she was sold away from her mama and papa. She was only ten. She's still here though, so I guess I'll just have to bear it like she did. Now I understand how many tears that must have cost her. Oh, this loathsome slavery; how can a merciful God allow it? I heard Dr. David is supposed to buy us. Let's just hope he didn't lie.

Sam

Tomorrow sister and baby girl go up on the block. I surely will miss Emily. She was always looking out for me and Reuben, making sure we got extra food or baking us a little something special. If I was a man, maybe I could do something to stop it, but I'm just a kid. Mama doesn't like me to say it, but someday I'm gonna get out of here and make it to Canada. I'll get a job up there and make enough money to buy Mama and Sam and Lizzie and even sister and baby. If I can't get out, sometimes I think I'll explode and kill somebody.

Lizzie

Sobbing, she says, "Mama, don't let Emmy and Mooshy leave me. Please don't. I need them. I need them right now. I can't go to sleep without Mooshy. Oh Mama please, please."

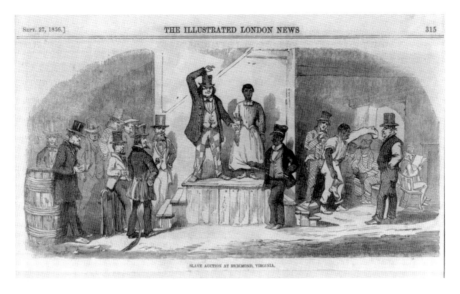

SLAVE AUCTION AT RICHMOND, VIRGINIA.

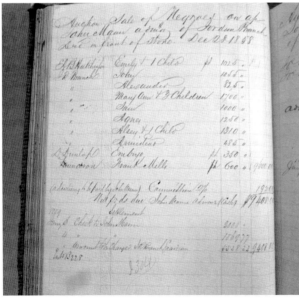

Above: A drawing of a slave auction in Richmond, Virginia, that appeared in the *Illustrated London News*, 1856. *Library of Congress.*

Left: Record of sale of Emily and Maria from the business records of Branch and Son, 1858. *Virginia Museum of History and Culture.*

The next day, an auction was held by Jordan Branch's brother Thomas in front of Branch and Son store in Petersburg to settle Jordan Branch's estate. Emily and Maria were sold away from their family for the princely sum of $1,025. At least the two of them were not separated. They were bought by a Mr. A.B. Hutchinson. MaryAnn and Emily's siblings were all bought back by the Branch family, so they stayed together. (We know that, through the years, Emily was in touch with MaryAnn, whose surname was Stokes. We know that Agnes's daughter Ellen Stokes signed as a witness on one of Emily's land transactions, and her daughter Maggie Stokes visited Emily in 1899.)

This type of sale was simply routine business, required to settle the estate, and was repeated thousands of times across the South. Families were torn asunder just like calves were sold from mother cows. The anguish it caused wasn't considered. This was an everyday occurrence. Thought was not given by the owners and brokers about the effects on the human beings who were being brokered. Let us examine the misery caused by this and other practices that caused family separations.

Chapter 4

FAMILY SEPARATIONS

Enslaved people lived with the constant threat that at any moment their family members might be sold or hired out to distant places, never to be seen again. Millions of people were separated. Although enslaved people could not legally marry, family ties formed nevertheless. A family might consist of a mother, father and their children; a group of orphaned or sold children; or a woman and her children by her owner. Regardless, family units were not honored. Individuals were considered capital assets and were bought and sold to suit their owners' financial designs. Even those whose owners had promised not to separate families could end up being sold or hired out to pay a debt, settle an estate, provide income for an orphan or widow or any other reason the masters chose. In many cases, the law required it.

Family separations were vividly recounted in an 1845 book written by an escaped slave named Lewis Clarke. Although he was from Kentucky, his narrative represents events throughout the South. The following is an excerpt from his book:

> *I never knew a whole family to live together till all were grown up in my life. There is almost always, in every family, some one or more keen and bright, or else sullen and stubborn slave, whose influence they are afraid of on the rest of the family, and such a one must take a walking ticket to the south.*
>
> *There are other causes of separation. The death of a large owner is the occasion usually of many families being broken up. Bankruptcy is another cause of separation, and the hard-heartedness of a majority of*

slave-holders another and a more fruitful cause than either or all the rest. Generally there is but little more scruple about separating families than there is with a man who keeps sheep in selling off the lambs in the fall. On one plantation where I lived, there was an old slave named Paris. He was from fifty to sixty years old, and a very honest and apparently pious slave. A slave-trader came along one day, to gather hands for the south. The old master ordered the waiter or coachman to take Paris into the back room pluck out all his gray hairs, rub his face with a greasy towel, and then had him brought forward and sold for a young man. His wife consented to go with him, upon a promise from the trader that they should be sold together, with their youngest child, which she carried in her arms. They left two behind them, who were only from four to six or eight years of age. The speculator collected his drove, started for the market, and, before he left the state, he sold that infant child to pay one of his tavern bills, and took the balance in cash....

There was a slave mother near where I lived, who took her child into the cellar and killed it. She did it to prevent being separated from her child. Another slave mother took her three children and threw them into a well, and then jumped in with them, and they were all drowned. Other instances I have frequently heard of. At the death of many and many a slave child, I have seen the two feelings struggling in the bosom of a mother—joy, that it was beyond the reach of the slave monsters, and the natural grief of a mother over her child. In the presence of the master, grief seems to predominate; when away from them, they rejoice that there is one whom the slave-killer will never torment.[8]

Richmond has its own stories. In 1815, a boy later to be known as Henry "Box" Brown was born enslaved in Louisa County, Virginia. When he was fifteen, his master died. In the settlement of the estate, Henry and his sister were given to his master's son and sent to live in Richmond—he to work in a tobacco factory, she to become a concubine to her master. He never saw the rest of his family again. Sometime later, Henry "married" with his master's permission, only to have his wife and children sold south one day while he was working. He never saw them again either. A year later, in 1849, having had enough, he packed himself in a crate and had himself shipped to an abolitionist society in Philadelphia. He knew he might die, and almost did, but he had gotten to the point that he didn't care.[9] Several books are available about Henry, including his autobiography. His story was not singular, though. Millions of people were separated.

"Hiring Out"

Another practice that separated families was "hiring out." This popular practice allowed less wealthy white Virginians, who had not the means to purchase people outright, to purchase their labor cheaply. For a small dollar amount, they could be masters and think of themselves as part of the superior economic and social class. The practice of hiring out created strong support among the lower-class whites for the slavocracy. Some owners bought slaves for the sole purpose of hiring them out, so they never labored on the owner's property. A skilled worker could bring great wealth to the master. Almost any kind of skill set could be had—field hands, carpenters, masons, blacksmiths, household workers, tobacco workers, waiters, wet nurses and so on.[10]

Advertisements for hiring out auctions appeared regularly in the Richmond papers. Some of them guaranteed the slaves would not be hired out for public works, because that work was usually so dangerous. People who were hired out were often treated with little regard for their health and safety, much as a rental house is often treated by tenants. The hirer might assign the hires to do dangerous jobs such as in mines or iron furnaces; work them overly hard; or refuse to feed and clothe them properly or provide any medical care. Because of this, many contracts required that the hirer provide insurance for the worker.

Often hiring brokers (like Jordan Branch's brother) advertised their services that would handle all aspects of hiring out, including making sure that the owners' properties would not be abused or put to work that was too

Left: An advertisement for public hiring of slaves that promises they will not be assigned to dangerous work. *Daily Dispatch*, December 24, 1855. *Library of Congress*.

Right: An advertisement by a broker who promises to watch over and protect hires from abuse to avoid heavy losses to owners. *Richmond Enquirer*, December 10, 1835. *Library of Congress*.

dangerous. Their pitch was that they could protect owners from financial loss if slaves were injured or killed. The necessity of this kind of service speaks to how dangerous the hired-out work could be.

Hirings were arranged at auctions and at large gatherings at a tavern or courthouse, where individual arrangements were made. Contracts began on January 1. The following is a newspaper account of such a gathering in Virginia from the *Alexandria Gazette* of January 2, 1861:

NEW YEARS DAY AT CATT'S

The annual gathering at Catt's Tavern, in the West End of this city, upon the first day of each year has long been the occasion of much interest to the good people of this neighborhood, either owning or hiring slave labor. To the negroes themselves, it is of course THE event of the year. Many years ago the crowds assembled there, were larger than now, and before the negroes dropped the turbans and linsey-woolsey for the cast off habiliments of the town, the spectacle presented was much more picturesque. The annual hirings still retain, however, many salient points of interest, and on yesterday the scene was unusually lively.

At an early hour of the day, crowds began to gather near the hiring ground, wagons with gaily dressed negroes drove up and dump'd their loads, numbers of darkeys came on foot, while whites in wagons, buggies, and on horse-back or by that species of locomotive apparatus known as "shank's mare" added to the crowd. Before noon some five hundred persons had gathered in the neighborhood. Cake dealers erected their stalls on dry places alongside the fences, or peddled their stores about in baskets among the negroes who were "flush of change" and merry as possible. By noon the business of the day had begun—the horses were fastened to the fences and the vehicles drawn up alongside, the cake stands were busy, the bars in full blast, the peripatetic confectioner doing an excellent business, and the holders of negroes chaffering with the hirers, or filling up the bonds which are the witnesses of the terms of hiring and evidence of the debt due next Christmas. So business among the whites went on all day, whilst mirth reigned among the negroes.

In a corner a conversation goes on as follows; "How does you Jim?"— "Fust rate Joe—whar does you go." "Oh, I goes to wait at first gentleman's table, very spectable situation—does you want a place." "Yes, but I'se no incubus good many people wants me, I shell be selection in my choosen." "Does you want to go to Pohick naberhood, I kin recommend a good family dar—bin wid un foar year." "No indeed—I shell patronize the town dis year."—"Well good bye."—"Good Bye, Darkie."

> *So the long day the sport continued. Tender hearted darkeys treated the female portion of culled-pussundom to ginger cakes, mint candy and gallantry, fighting whiskey exhibited its power in sundry bloodless encounters; darkeys found masters and by night the work was accomplished and hiring day over.*
>
> *Some three hundred and fifty negroes were hired at rates similar to those of last year, viz.: men $80@$110; women, $40@$80: children, $25@$70.*

This lighthearted account in the white newspaper paints a picture of a bucolic, country fair type of gathering, with jovial, moneyed Negroes coming to negotiate their own futures, merrily singing and dancing all the while. There is no mention that they might not have seen their families for the entire previous year and would not see them for another year. Only the last sentence shows the stark realities of the money their masters would receive for their labors and also that children were being hired out, often separate from their families. We also wonder how the writer of this piece decided how to spell the words the hirees spoke. Did he assume they would know how to spell the word patronize, but not neighborhood? Or was the entire conversation contrived, with the intent of making them look crude and ridiculous, but in charge of their own futures?

The description above contrasts sharply with the remembrances of a young boy who was hired out:

> *My owner hired me out to some poor people that lived in the country…when I was only about 6 years old. They hired me to nurse, but I had to nurse, cook, chop in the fields, chop wood, bring water, wash, iron and in general just do everything. On Sundays they would go to church and leave me there to clean the house and cook dinner. When they got back home from church, I always had the meal ready because if it wasn't ready, I knew what was coming. I didn't get any whippings because I always did what I was told, in a hurry.*[11]

Hiring contracts started in January and ended right before Christmas. Standard forms were available that stated the conditions of the hiring, such as what clothes, food and healthcare must be provided. Should the hireling expire during the period, rent would be prorated. We found a hiring-out contract for "the negro man named Will." He was hired out by David Moore for seventy-two dollars for one year from Robert Bollings of Petersburg on

March 18, 1814. Will was to be furnished with two good osnaburg shirts, one good double homespun jacket, one pair of good thick overalls, one good pair of shoes, one pair of stockings, one good hat and one good Dutch blanket. The lease went from Christmas 1814 to Christmas 1815. There was nothing mentioned in the contract regarding food, medical care, housing or indeed anything to do with the maintenance of Will's health or well-being. He died on August 2, 1815. The rent was prorated appropriately, and Bollings had to issue a refund. There is no mention of how Will died, only concern for prorating the rent.

An enslaved person with a particularly valuable skill did have some advantage. He might be allowed to select among prospective hirers, hire himself out and actually have a measure of independent living, as long as he paid a yearly required dollar amount to his owner. If he managed to earn additional income, he might save it and eventually purchase himself. If hired out in a city, especially a port city, the chance of escape improved. Two famous escapees, Frederick Douglass and Anthony Burns, took advantage of that kind of opportunity. This advantage was not lost on some locals who thought the enslaved were being given too much control over themselves. Here is an opinion in the *Daily Dispatch* of December 18, 1856:

Hiring by Auction: It would be wise policy in the owners of slaves, to hire them out by auction in future, instead of following the old plan of allowing them to select their own homes, and thus become masters instead of servants. For some years past our tobacco manufacturers have been compelled, in order to secure labor, first to purchase the consent of the negroes to live with them, and then to hire them of their owners, and, in order to do so, have allowed the servants to dictate their own terms as to the amount of board money to be given, the extent of daily labor to be performed, and the price to be paid for such overwork as they may feel disposed to do. Such a policy has already proved to be most injurious to the slaves themselves, and will eventuate in their becoming entirely worthless if persisted in. By adopting the system of hiring them out by auction, the owner can state the kind of labor at which his servant is to be employed, and to arrange the bond as to make it obligatory on the hirer to keep him at certain labor. If a negro is intended for a tobacco factory, field hand, cook or driver he can be put on the block for any particular employment, and thus insure good homes for his property. This subject is worthy the attention of slave owners, and would prove highly beneficial to the public at large, if carried out.

People who were hired out might not know where their next job would be. It could be different from month to month or year to year. Usually, they were allowed to return to their homes at Christmas for a week, not knowing if their loved ones would still be there. On January 1, they would be gone again. Women with small children were less desirable, so the children would often be hired out separately as soon as they were able to perform some service.

Taken together, the sales and hiring out of enslaved people separated untold numbers of families. After the Civil War, thousands of people took to the roads, advertised in newspapers and took whatever other means they could to try to find their families. Most never did. On January 17, 1895, the following advertisement appeared in the *Christian Recorder* in Philadelphia, thirty years after the end of the Civil War. This woman had gone all that time never knowing where her family was.

> *INFORMATION WANTED OF my husband and son. We parted at Richmond, VA, in 1860. My son's name was Jas. Monroe Holmes; my husband's name was Frank Holmes. My son was sold in Richmond, Va. I don't know where they carried him to. My husband was not sold. I left him in Richmond, Va. and I have five children, Henry, Gabriel, Charles, Dortha and Jacob were sold to a trader who lived in Texas. I am now old, and don't think that I shall be here long and would like to see them before I die. Any information concerning them will be thankfully received by Eliza Holmes, Flatonia, Fayette Co., Texas.*

Chapter 5

DAVID WINFREE

L et us now introduce the Jones children's great-grandfather, David Winfree. We have told you about Emily and Maria's sale to Hutchinson. Emily might have been pregnant at the time of the sale. She had a second child, Elizabeth Winfree, in 1859 or 1860. Eighteen months after the sale, they were owned by David Winfree in Chesterfield County, Virginia.

David Winfree was born around 1814 to James Wiley and Lucy Patteson Winfree. The Winfrees had been in Virginia since the 1600s and the Pattesons since the 1700s. Both had acquired land, affluence and influence and were firmly entrenched in the slavocracy.

THE PATTESONS

David Winfree's maternal grandfather was David Patteson, born in 1746 in New Kent County, Virginia. At one time, he was the plantation manager at William Byrd III's Falls Plantation (later Manchester). He married heiress Elizabeth Ann Jordan of Amelia, Virginia. She was the granddaughter of Henry Stokes. Patteson bought several pieces of land from Byrd III in Henrico County and Manchester. He also owned a 993-acre plantation, called Laurel Meadow, in Chesterfield County. Patteson was a lieutenant in Robert Goode's Company during the Revolutionary War and was at the siege and surrender at Yorktown. He later became commandant of the Chesterfield Militia, and in 1794, he ordered the militia to guard Mayo's Bridge across the James River and stop the traffic to prevent the smallpox epidemic spreading from Richmond to Manchester.[12] He also served in the General Assembly, and in 1788, he voted to ratify the United States Constitution at the Virginia Constitutional Convention. A devout man, he was a reader and vestryman for the Episcopal church in Manchester and Falling Creek. Over the years, he served as both justice of the peace and sheriff of Chesterfield County. David Patteson died in 1821.[13]

David and Elizabeth Jordan Patteson had nine children. Two of their daughters married into families important to this story. Their daughter Mary married Thomas Branch and was the mother of Jordan Branch (Emily's owner and David Winfree's brother-in-law). Jordan also owned MaryAnn Stokes (who we discussed regarding Emily's birth). Possibly, he inherited her through his mother's family, the Stokeses. The Branches were also an old Virginia family, arriving about 1619. The other daughter of the Pattesons important to this story is Lucy. It seems she was a rude and haughty teenager. While enrolled in a school run by Thomas Upshaw, her behavior was so bad that Upshaw finally told her parents that either he be allowed to discipline her with a tighter rein or he would discharge her from his school. They apparently chose the latter and brought her home. Subsequently, Upshaw sued them for payment for the time she was in attendance.[14] We do not know the outcome of the suit. Her importance to this story is that she later married James Wiley Winfree and became David Winfree's mother. We have no further accounts of her behavior. The Branch family and the Winfree family continued to intertwine.

The Winfrees

Like the Pattesons, the Winfrees first settled in New Kent County. Records from St. Peter's Church have them there as early as 1688. By the early 1700s, the Winfree family held large tracts of land and many slaves in Chesterfield County. James Wiley Winfree (David Winfree's father) was born in 1781. He became a prominent citizen in the Richmond area. According to the *Richmond Enquirer*, he was a director of the Bank of Virginia, raced his own horses at the Broad Rock Races and had extensive property holdings,

Left: David Winfree's father, James Wiley Winfree. *Right*: David Winfree's mother, Lucy Patteson Winfree. *Chesterfield Historical Society.*

including a large plantation on the James River in Buckingham County. He married the above-mentioned Lucy Patteson in 1809, and they had five children who survived infancy: William, David, Lucy, Martha Elizabeth and Sarah Susanna.

Young David and his siblings grew up in a house known locally as "British Camp" that was situated off Broad Rock Road in Southside Richmond near where the VA Hospital is today. It got that moniker during the Revolutionary War, when it was used as headquarters by Major General William Phillips, and his soldiers made camp around the house. The house was still serviceable in 1965, when it was dismantled and moved to Goochland County, west of Richmond. It is now a private residence.[15]

All three of David's sisters married into the Branch family via their mother's sister, Aunt Mary Branch. His sister Lucy married Mary's son Jordan. His sister Martha Elizabeth married Mary's grandson William T. Lithgow. His sister Sarah Susanna married Mary's grandson Dr. Syndenham Walke. He and his father, John Walke, had a medical practice at Physic Hill in Chesterfield County. In addition to treating patients, they also examined enslaved people brought there for medical assessments prior to auctions. There is a large flat rock said to be a "slave auction block" at the historical mansion Magnolia Grange, across from the Chesterfield County Courthouse, that is thought to have originally been in front of the house at

The home of David Winfree's sister and brother-in-law, Sarah and Syndenham Walke, as it looks today, on Bainbridge Street, one block over from Emily's home. *Authors' photograph.*

Physic Hill. The Walkes later lived on Bainbridge Street in Manchester, two blocks from Emily.[16]

David attended undergraduate school at the University of Virginia. In July 1836, the *Richmond Enquirer* reported that he earned high academic honors in materia medica (pharmacology), physiology and chemistry. In 1838, he graduated from the University of Pennsylvania, where he received his medical degree.[17] Syndenham Walke, his brother-in-law, was at the same medical school, about two years ahead of David. We have found no records indicating that David ever practiced medicine.

The Winfrees had many enslaved people, and between 1853 and 1860, David fathered at least seven children with women owned by his family. He would have been about forty at the time. He fathered Andrew, Rachel, Sarah and one unnamed child with an enslaved woman named Agnes; Eliza, by one named Judith; an unnamed daughter by one named Susan; and a son, Hampton, by an unnamed woman.[18] The family had every legal right to sell these children, but we don't know if they did so. We have found no records to indicate what became of these children.

Slave Breeding

The practice of impregnation of enslaved women by white men was commonplace and was not just gratification of lust. It was part of the purposeful "breeding" of enslaved people that was the norm in the slavocracy, and it is worth further exploration.

Young enslaved women were considered breeding livestock, and their children increased an owner's wealth more than any crop they might produce as laborers. A planter's wealth, status, political influence and credit worthiness were all measured by the number of people he owned, and a single female could produce many marketable children during her fertile life span. Auction houses advertised young "likely wenches" of breeding age (around fourteen years). Masters often paired off particular enslaved men and women they owned, just as they would their livestock. Particularly strong, robust male slaves were sometimes "rented" out to neighboring plantations as studs. A former slave related the following story:

> *"Joe was 'bout seven feet tall an' was de breedinges' n----- in Virginia. Didn't have no work to do, jus' stay 'round de quarters sunnin' hisself 'til a call come fo' him. 'Member once ole Marsa hired him out to a white man what lived down in Suffolk. Dey come an' got him on a Friday. Dey brung him back Monday mo'nin. Dey say dat de next year dere was sebenteen little black babies bo'n at dat place in Suffolk, all on de same day." Interview with ex-slave West Turner.*[19]

Even people such as Thomas Jefferson, whose apologists maintain that he was against slavery, were actively breeding slaves. A clear example of his thinking is shown in the following excerpt from one of his many writings on the subject. It is taken from a letter he wrote on January 17, 1819, to Joel Yancey, his farm manager, regarding recent deaths among his slaves:

> *The deaths of the grown ones seem ascribable to natural causes, but the loss of 5 little ones in a year induces me to fear that the overseers do not permit the women to devote as much time as is necessary to the care of their children: that they view their labor as the first object and the raising of their children but as secondary. I consider the labor of a breeding woman as no object, and that a child raised every two years is of more profit than the crop of the best laboring man. In this as in all other cases, providence has made our interests and our duties coincide perfectly. Women too are destroyed by*

exposure to wet at certain periodical indispositions to which nature has subjected them. With respect therefore to our women and their children I must pray you to inculcate upon the overseers that it is not their labor, but their increase which is the consideration with us.[20]

As tobacco growing depleted the soils of Virginia, planters had shifted to crops like small grains. Growing those crops was not as labor intensive as growing tobacco, and the result was a surplus of enslaved people. That caused a devaluation of their price. To prevent further devaluation from the importation of Africans, in 1778, under Governor Jefferson, Virginia banned their importation into the commonwealth. The United States government also banned their importation, but that law was not to go into effect until 1808. In 1803, Jefferson, as president, obtained the Louisiana Purchase from France. This opened up huge new territory, and the movement of the plantation economy into the newly acquired lands brought a huge new market for laborers. This raised the value of enslaved people again and encouraged Virginia slave breeders. To ensure that Virginians would profit from this opportunity, Jefferson immediately pushed a law through Congress that prohibited those who settled in the new territories from buying imported people and required them to buy only from domestic markets, such as Virginia. This effectively shut down the sale of imported people five years prior to the planned U.S. ban and provided Virginia and other slave-breeding states an immediate, exclusive market. The result was an increase in breeding.[21]

Chapter 6

DAVID AND EMILY IN CHESTERFIELD COUNTY

*T*he earliest record we have of David and Emily together is the 1860 Chesterfield County Slave Census, when they were living on his farm with her daughters Maria and Elizabeth (Bettie). According to the census, Bettie was less than a year old at the time. We don't know when David had purchased them or if he was Bettie's father. Emily was to have three more children while she was with David. In 1862, a son, Walter David Winfree, was born. In 1865, James Wiley Winfree (David's father's name) arrived. There is every reason to believe they were David's sons. Emily's jobs were cook, washer and ironer. Maria was by now about seven and probably helped with the chores. The Civil War had started in 1861, and life was becoming difficult in Virginia. As the war dragged on, inflation was rampant; there were bread riots in Richmond; the enslaved were being impressed to work on the earthworks surrounding the city; and some were running away. Confederate-issued money was becoming worthless. Property was losing its value. As things got worse for the South, owners of enslaved people must have realized that, if the war was lost, virtually all of their wealth would vanish. Perhaps that's why David tried, in 1863, to sell some of his property. He was not successful. Thankfully, none of Emily's children were sold.

On June 17, 1864, David enlisted in the Confederate army as a private in Company G of the First Regiment, Virginia Reserves, known as Fairnholt's Reserves.[22] His brother-in-law, John Lithgow, also joined. Most of that regiment was captured at the Battle of Sailer's Creek during Lee's retreat to

Appomattox in April 1865. However, David was not on that retreat because he was in the hospital. On December 23, 1864, at a Confederate army hospital in Farmville, Virginia, a Confederate physician saw David and wrote the following: "Ordered here by surgeon of regiment. Syphilitic rheumatism of many years standing. Exceedingly delicate and frail constitution, is fifty years of age. Recommended for light duty and to report to Surgeon F.G. Hancock in charge of Jackson Hospital in Richmond."[23]

David was furloughed for sixty days and then discharged. During that period in history, there was little that could be done for David's condition. Syphilis was very common and was a sentence of prolonged suffering and sometimes horrible disfigurement. Antibiotics had not yet been discovered, and the standard treatment was with various mercury ointments, which we know now are toxic. Today, syphilis is very simply treated with penicillin. This illness "of many years standing" could explain David's absence at Emily's sale and his attempts to sell his land. It also raises the concern for us that Emily and her children fathered by David might have also been syphilitic. It seems they were not, as all lived past the age of sixty. There are times in the records when the whole family was ill, but there is no way of knowing the cause.

Doubtless realizing his death was imminent, David started to take care of his affairs. On February 23, 1865, he put his entire Chesterfield farm (548.5 acres) up for auction. Part of the farm was productive crop land, and part was wooded. There was a house and all necessary outbuildings. The reality of the dire situation is reflected by the fact that he felt compelled to assure potential buyers that the fighting between the Union and Confederate armies would probably not get as far as his property. This brings into sharp focus the unsettled situation in the Richmond area.

That spring, the Confederacy was falling apart. Although David implies fighting would not occur near the farm, Petersburg was only twenty-five miles away. The Battles of Hatcher's Run, Five Forks, Sailer's Creek and finally Appomattox were all over the newspapers. Petersburg had been evacuated by the Confederates. Emily must have been concerned for her family. We don't know what their situation was. They might have been evacuated with the Branches. We wonder if her relationship with David was such that he allowed her to find or visit them. Surely, she realized that the South was losing the war and that, when it lost, she would be free. She also had to have known the seriousness of David's illness. Did she welcome or fear what was certainly coming? Would she and her children be put out to fend for themselves? That is what happened to millions of people.

VERY VALUABLE FARM OF FIVE HUNDRED AND FORTY-EIGHT AND A HALF ACRES, IN CHESTERFIELD COUNTY, SIX MILES FROM RICHMOND, AND GRIST AND SAW-MILL, AND FIFTEEN THOUSAND FEET OF INCH PLANK, FOR SALE AT AUCTION.—Will be sold at auction, on the premises, on MONDAY, the 27th of February, at 12 o'clock M., the valuable FARM of five hundred and forty-eight and a half acres, in Chesterfield county, the present residence of Dr. D. C. Winfree. It lies on Falling creek, within six miles of Richmond; two hundred and ninety-five acres cleared, the balance heavily wooded and well timbered, being, probably, the largest body of wood land in any one tract so near the city. The land is in a high state of cultivation, and much of it has been limed and clovered. It is well watered and healthy. There is a mill site on the place, and the walls of the mill and a part of the remains stand. The improvements consist of an excellent brick dwelling, with four rooms above the basement, and all necessary out-houses, and a large ice-house filled with ice.

After the sale of the farm, we will sell a SAW and GRIST MILL, on Falling creek, a never-failing stream, with four acres of land attached, in good repair. Also, fifteen thousand feet of INCH PLANK, and one LOG WAGON, in good order, and a handsome set of DOUBLE BUGGY HARNESS.

TERMS: At sale.

GRUBBS & WILLIAMS, Auctioneers.

fe 16—cod6t

It is proper to state that the above property has not been, nor is likely to be, depredated upon by either army, as it is located in a section sufficiently remote from the probable lines of their operations.

fe 21   G. & W., Auctioneers.

Left: An advertisement for sale of David Winfree's farm in Chesterfield County. *Daily Dispatch*, February 23, 1865. *Library of Congress*.

Below: An advertisement by David Winfree for an overseer. The washer, ironer and cook is most likely Emily. *Daily Dispatch*, March 10, 1865. *Library of Congress*.

WANTED.— I wish to employ an OVERSEER for the balance of the year. None need apply unless well qualified for the business and exempt from the army. I have a very superior WASHER, IRONER and COOK, with four small children, for whom I will pay a reasonable amount for the balance of the year.

mh 7—1aw2w   D. C. WINFREE.

No buyer came forth for the farm. Three weeks later, on March 10, David advertised in the *Daily Dispatch* for an overseer for the rest of the year. In the ad, he states that he has an excellent washer, cook and ironer with four small children. We must remind the reader that these children were property that could legally have been sold at any time but were not, although David was in debt.

We next meet Emily and David in 1866. The South had, indeed, lost the war, so Emily and the children were free, but they were still with David, and another child, Henry Winfree, had been born. On March 14 of that year, in spite of his debts, David bought for Emily a small house in Manchester for $800. (The deed is provided in Appendix I.) That purchase speaks to his feelings of responsibility, if not affection or love, for Emily and her/

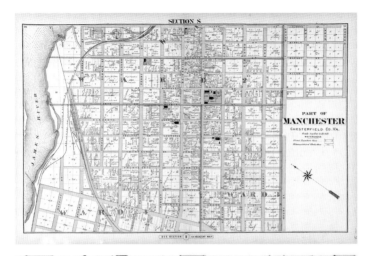

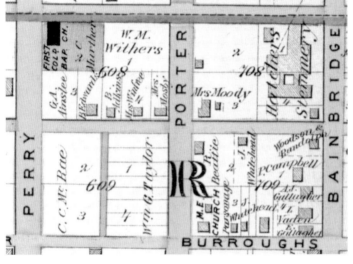

Top: Beer's map of Manchester, 1876. *Library of Congress.*

Bottom: An enlargement of the section of Beer's map that shows Mrs. Winfree's lot near Eighth and Porter, 1876. *Library of Congress.*

their children. The property was fifty feet from Porter Street on Allen Street, which later became Eighth Street, which later became Commerce Avenue.

Two months later, on May 29, he granted her a 109.5-acre tract of his farm. It was the poorer part of the farm and did not include the house or outbuildings. It was mostly wooded. (That deed is provided in Appendix II.)

David gave Emily exclusive rights to both properties. She could keep or sell them. She could rent them out. She could pass them down to her children or to any other persons she named in a will. If Emily died without naming any heirs, the properties were to revert back to David. David also named a trustee, A.A. Allen, for Emily, to look out for her interests because she could not read or write. However, in the long run, having a trustee cost her. She was not allowed to act alone in any transactions related to the properties but was required to "unite with the trustee," whom she had to pay each time she went to court. It was he who had to petition the court each and every time she wanted to cut timber, buy or sell property, move money or do anything else related to the properties. After Allen died, the court appointed J.M. Moody, who also died. James M. Purdue, the administrator for Moody, temporarily took over the duties of trustee until H.W. Bransford was appointed. After he died, P.V. Cogbill was appointed. He was her last trustee.

Chapter 7

DAVID'S DEATH

O n March 20, 1867, David Winfree died. He and Emily had lived together (or at least on the same property) for several years and had three, four or five children together. For the last two of those years, Emily was not enslaved to him, but she did not leave. Likely she had tended to him in his sickness. What was the scene at his death? Was she at his bedside? Or were his white family members there, leaving her to stand aside? Were the children there? What had they called him? Was he Daddy, or Master? His funeral service was at the Methodist church in Manchester. Was Emily there, up in the balcony with the "coloreds"? What must she have been thinking? Imagine this scene.

As the family sat down to their supper, the children were frightened by the stricken look on their mama's face. They had never seen her like that before, and it was unnerving. Maria, the oldest, said, "What's wrong, Mama?" "Children, I got some bad news today. Your father has died. You know he's been sick a long time. I went over to see him right at the end." What she didn't tell the children were the final words David had spoken to her, when she went up to the bedside. He was so weak that he couldn't lift his head, and she had to lean over the bed, her ear next to his lips. Still, she could hardly hear him when he said, "I'm sorry." Emily had not spoken, having no reply to voice. She had been with David, had been owned by David, for many years. She had children by him yet had never actually known him. They had never spoken about their relationship. This dying man had kept his "wife" and children as chattel but in the end took steps to provide and care for them after they were free. He had bought the house for her even though he was in debt; given her the land in the country; and given her money all along. Maybe he felt guilty and was making

In this city, on Wednesday morning, 20th instant, Dr DAVID C. WINFREE, in the fifty third
year of his age.
 His funeral services will take place THIS DAY
(Thursday) at 11 o'clock A. M. from the Methodist
church, Manchester. His friends and those of the
family are invited to attend.
 Petersburg papers please copy.

Notice of David Winfree's death. *Daily Dispatch*, March 21, 1867. *Library of Congress.*

amends. *Maybe he really did care. What difference did all of that make now? What could she buy with "I'm sorry"? That was nothing but history, and her only reality now was that she had five small children to feed and look after. She had no time to ponder matters that no longer mattered. She had to look forward.*

She willed her thoughts back into the room. "There will be a service for him tomorrow morning at eleven at the Methodist church. We will go." The children were disoriented. The three boys hardly knew who their father was. Walter was only four, James and Henry even younger, when they moved into this cottage, and their father didn't live here with them, although they saw him occasionally. The girls were older. They had lived on the farm with him and remembered him. They didn't understand anything about his relationship with their mother, but they had missed seeing him since they moved here. Maria's only question was, "What should we wear? We don't have anything nice." "We will look the best we can and make sure we are clean and respectable looking. I will have to go over now to tell Mrs. Langford I will be late tomorrow."

The next morning, the family walked over to the Methodist church together. They were as well dressed as their circumstances allowed. The boys were scrubbed clean and told to be on their best behavior. Eleven-year-old Maria was doing her best to keep them corralled. She wanted so much to help, but they never listened to her. Although the family had done their best, the little procession still compared shabbily to the white congregants. David's other family greeted them at the door and politely but pointedly showed them the stairs to the "colored" section in the balcony. Emily donned her subservient smile reserved for whites, thanked them and headed up the stairs with the children. The church seemed very grand compared to her usual church. It had stained-glass windows, solid mahogany pews, a huge golden crucifix behind the altar and patterned carpeting throughout the sanctuary. From the balcony, they could see the casket up at the altar, but it was closed. This was the closest Emily would get to the father of her children. The preacher came in and asked everybody to open with a prayer. The service dragged on, seemingly forever, and Emily just couldn't stay focused on the preacher's words. She was so worried about their situation and distracted by James and Henry's constant squirming. After several unsuccessful attempts to quiet them, she knew people were starting to look, so finally Emily told Maria to take all the children home. She stayed until the end, said a final silent prayer, waited for all the white people to pass first and then started to head back. Before she could get out of the church, it started to sprinkle a bit. She had on her only shoes and her cheap hat. She had stuffed fresh newspaper in both shoes to cover the holes in the soles, but that wouldn't stand up to a downpour. As she headed out, the rain started coming down in buckets, and by the time she got to the end of the block, the newspaper was a soggy mess. Her hat was soaked, and blue dye was running from the cheap straw flower on top and tinting the rain that was running down her face, so that it looked as if she was crying blue tears. How fitting, she thought. She stopped and took off the hat and looked at it. "I wonder if it can be saved. It's the only one I have, so I'll have to try; maybe I can make a new flower for it." She put the hat under her arm. Then she took off the shoes, put them under the other arm and continued on home, barefoot. By the time she got there, her clothes, her body and her mood were all thoroughly wilted.

When Emily arrived at the house, she just stood there at the front steps in a puddle up to her ankles. She contemplated the peeling paint, the deteriorating shingles and the broken gutter. David had said he would have them fixed, but now she didn't know. She climbed the steps, carefully avoiding the rotten one, and opened the door. What she beheld was chaos. Walter had tied James to the table leg and was tickling him. The table had gotten dragged halfway across the room and knocked over, along with the best chair. Luckily, James, the table and the chair seemed to be unbroken. Bettie was holding Henry in her arms, trying to get him to eat a piece of cornbread, which he was spitting on the floor. Maria was trying to untie James while Walter was jumping on her back. Emily stood there, bare-headed and barefoot, and watched her girls struggling with the boys. Emily knew Maria, knew that she would do her best, but she wondered if she really could manage it. She was a strong girl and was trying very hard, but was she really up to this? "We're gonna have to do better than this," she thought. She got out of her wet clothes and put the shoes and hat aside to dry. She helped her daughters, and finally, they got the boys quieted down and fed and hustled them into the other room to nap. Emily sat down at the now righted table and motioned for Maria and Bettie to sit. "I'm afraid things are going to change for us. We won't be getting the money from your father anymore, so I will have to take another job. Maria, you're eleven now. You will have to run the house, and Bettie, you must help her. I know the boys are a handful, but we have to teach them to help out too. We will face these hard times together. All those years we were slaves, I lived with the fear that you children would be sold away from me, and I would have had nothing to say about it. Now I do have something to say about it, and I say we will do whatever we have to in order to stay together. We don't have much, hardly anything really, but if you can promise me you will do your best, I will do my best, and together we will make it. Can you do that, girls?" Maria got that determined look on her face that, years later, her grandchildren would come to know so well and said, "Yes, Mama. I promise." So did Bettie.

We shall never know the true relationship between and David and Emily Winfree. They were father and mother but not husband and wife. For most of their time together, they were owner and owned, but for the rest of her life, Emily was called Mrs. Winfree, and she was listed as a widow on her death certificate. Emily's great-granddaughter Emily Grace remembers hearing as a child stories about David and Emily. She knows that her own mother and her Grandma "Moosh" (Maria) adored Emily and often talked about how much David had cared for her. Maria was ten or eleven when David died. She would have remembered him. While marriage between former slaves and masters was very rare, it was not unheard of and not illegal in Virginia for a few years during Reconstruction. If their relationship was in fact a loving one, they were tragically entangled in the web of the Virginia slavocracy. Being from a very prominent family, David would have been totally ostracized for loving a slave, although not for fathering her children. It was entirely acceptable for a white man to have sexual relations with an African American woman, but to marry one was a different matter—not allowed! There is no record of David having ever married anybody. Was that because of his feelings for Emily? Nobody can answer these questions for us; all the players in this tragedy are gone. So our natural longing for answers remains unfulfilled.

The timing of David's death after, rather than prior to, the end of the war was critical to Emily and her children, because David died in debt. Had he died prior to the end of the war, she and the children could have been sold by the heirs to pay those debts. This happened to an untold number of people throughout the South. Even those who had been owned by people who did not believe in separating families, or who had planned for their people to be freed after their deaths, often ended up sold and separated. Although most of David's debts were owed to family members, we do not know what might have happened.

Whatever the answers to the above questions may be, David's death was devastating for Emily. If they truly cared for each other, she had the emotional loss. But the most critical question was how she was to live. She was thrown into independence with five children and no means of support. Her oldest child was eleven years old. She could not read or write, had spent almost her whole life enslaved and knew only domestic work. Even if she had been educated, only domestic work was available to African American women. Perhaps David's relatives helped her. Documents we present later indicate that she was well acquainted and friendly with some of the family members. But the whole South, especially Virginia, was devastated by the war, and perhaps the family had financial burdens as well.

There were many more trials and tribulations yet to befall Emily and her children. We cannot possibly comprehend them or truly appreciate what it took for her to come through it with her family alive, intact and ultimately very successful, unless we have a good understanding of what her world was like after the Civil War. Therefore, it is necessary for us to now take a major digression from our story to discuss what was happening around Emily in the years after the war.

Chapter 8

BROKEN PROMISES

LOST HOPE

So here we have Emily and her family. She is free and independent—
no longer enslaved. Now she can get an education, be paid for her
labor, marry if she wishes and enjoy all the rights and opportunities
promised in the Declaration of Independence and the new amendments to
the United States Constitution. But somehow, she continued to live in abject
poverty. Where did she go wrong? What poor choices did she make? Was she
just shiftless and lazy? Was she licentious or wasteful? What went wrong was
that, despite the promises and lofty language, Virginia and the rest of the
South hurtled into Reconstruction and then Jim Crow and, with malevolent
purpose, systematically quashed the aspirations of African Americans. Freed
Virginians were betrayed by everybody: presidents, the United States Army,
Congress and even the Supreme Court. Most of all, they were betrayed by
the Commonwealth of Virginia. Except for one brief shining moment, the
South entered a period during which African Americans were systematically
deprived of life, liberty and the pursuit of happiness in the most horrific
ways imaginable.

Most Americans are ignorant of what happened in their country for more
than one hundred years after the Civil War. Those years have been passed
over or glossed over in public school books, and even today, it takes some
effort to piece together everything that happened. Most Americans are aware
of the Civil War, though they may not know why or when it was fought.
They also know who Martin Luther King Jr. was and are familiar with the
civil rights movement. What happened in the intervening century remains
a gaping hole in the public consciousness. The tragedy of this ignorance is

that it leaves us with no understanding of the root causes of the strained race relationships we have today and ill-prepared to develop remedies. It is worth the effort to herein describe the confluence of factors that kept Emily in ignorance and poverty and caused her descendants to finally abandon Virginia and take their many talents elsewhere.

Presidential Reconstruction

On April 4, 1865, after Confederate forces evacuated Richmond, Abraham Lincoln arrived. Those who had been enslaved rejoiced in the streets. After two and a half centuries, their time had come. Hopes soared. Now, finally, they would be treated as citizens and could enjoy the fruits of their labor, own their own property instead of being property, legally marry and a whole host of other things they had been denied for so long. Lincoln had signed the Emancipation Proclamation; he had pushed the Thirteenth Amendment, which abolished slavery in the Unites States, through Congress. He wanted to heal the nation. Eleven days later, he was dead, shot in the head by a bitter Confederate sympathizer. Thus began a shameful era in the South during which whites systematically, step by step, ensured that the former enslaved people would remain in a state of servitude and abject poverty for over one hundred more years. The white supremacists subjugated the African American population by means of criminalization, forced labor, terror, intimidation, segregation and disenfranchisement. Would it have happened if Lincoln had not been murdered? We shall never know.

White southerners were bitter. They could not accept either the loss of the social hierarchy or the loss of free labor they had enjoyed prior to the Civil War. This bitterness has outlasted every attempt at healing and is advanced by white supremacist organizations still today. In 1996, six hundred Richmonders, waving Confederate flags, loudly protested the unveiling of a statue of African American tennis great Arthur Ashe on Richmond's Monument Avenue. In 2003, the idea of erecting a statue of Lincoln and his son Tad in Richmond provoked petitions, writings equating the idea with putting a statue of Hitler in Israel, street protests and attempts to disrupt the unveiling ceremony. In 2017, an armed white supremacist rally in Charlottesville, protesting the removal of a statue of Robert E. Lee from a public park, resulted in murder. The horrible legacy of slavery is alive and well in the Commonwealth of Virginia.

The new amendments to the U.S. Constitution gave the rights of citizens to the freedmen. If southern whites let this stand, they would lose the strict social and economic hierarchy they had so masterfully maintained for centuries. They were having none of it. The man who replaced Lincoln as president, Andrew Johnson, an ex–slave holder from Tennessee, was sympathetic. He ushered the South into a period called Presidential Reconstruction, which incorporated his own, rather than Lincoln's, ideas about the limited ways in which things should be managed. Other than the requirements that southern states abolish slavery, repudiate secession and abrogate their debts, he gave them a free hand in managing their own affairs. Whites who had fought against the Union were pardoned and left in charge of their state and local governments. The Thirteenth Amendment had a dangerous loophole. It abolished slavery and involuntary servitude, *except* for punishment of a crime. The entire South rushed through that loophole and wasted no time in passing a series of laws known as the "Black codes." In Virginia, vagrancy became a crime and petty crimes were elevated to felonies. Even trivial acts or a wrong word could land a freedman in prison. These laws, enforced by former Confederates, served to criminalize African Americans and thus provide a free or very cheap workforce. On January 15, 1866, Virginia passed the Vagrancy Act.

For two and a half centuries, descendants of the first Africans brought to Virginia in 1619 had not owned themselves or their labor. They could not choose the labor they performed and received no wages for that labor. For the most part, the jobs to which they were assigned were menial. Now, suddenly, they were free, and they expected to choose the jobs they performed and to be compensated fairly for their labor. Instead, they found that they were forced to accept whatever labor was offered, at whatever compensation was offered. This began immediately. In May and June 1865, right after the surrender, freedmen who had come to Richmond were rounded up by Union troops, held in former slave jails and later sent back to the rural areas to work on the plantations.[24] In many areas, white employers had already made agreements to pay freedmen lower-than-normal wages. If freedmen refused to work for these depressed wages, they were fodder for the new Vagrancy Act. For boys and men, this meant no choice of employment other than menial labor. For girls and women, it meant the drudgery of domestic work. The Vagrancy Act was very verbose and redundant, so we shall edit it for the sake of clarity:

Be it enacted by the General Assembly that:

Section 1. Overseers of the poor or other officers having charge of the poor, or the police or a county or corporation, are empowered and required, if they discover any vagrant within their respective counties or corporations, to report it to any justice of the peace of their county or corporation and to get a warrant to arrest the vagrant. If he is found to be a true vagrant the justice shall order him to be employed in labor for any term not exceeding three months, and to be hired out for the best wages that can be procured, the wages to be given to his family. If he runs away, he shall be apprehended taken back to the hirer, and one month added to his sentence, and the hirer shall be allowed to work said vagrant, confined with ball and chain. If the hirer will not take him back, he shall be taken to the work house and be worked for the benefit of the county or corporation, confined with ball and chain, for the period for which he would have had to serve his late employer. If there is no work house, or no work going on, then the vagrant will be delivered to any person who will take charge of him and who will get his services for free. If nobody can be found, he will be sent to the county jail and fed on bread and water.

The following described persons shall be liable to the penalties imposed by law upon vagrants:

First—All persons who shall unlawfully return into any county or corporation whence they have been legally removed.

Second—All persons who, not having wherewith to maintain themselves and their families, live idly and without employment, and refuse to work for the usual and common wages given to other laborers in the like work in the place where they then are.

Third—All persons who shall refuse to perform the work which shall be allotted to them by the overseers of the poor as aforesaid.

Fourth—All persons going about from door to door, or placing themselves in streets, highways or other roads, to beg alms, and all other persons wandering abroad and begging unless disabled or incapable of labor.

Fifth—All persons who shall come from any place without this commonwealth to any place within it, and shall be found loitering and residing therein, and shall follow no labor, trade, occupation or business, and have no visible means of subsistence, and can give no reasonable account of themselves or their business in such place.

All costs and expenses incurred shall be paid out of the hire of such vagrant, if sufficient; and if not sufficient, the deficiency shall be paid by the county or corporation.

Section 2. All freedmen, free Negroes, and mulattos in this state over the age of eighteen years found on the second Monday in January 1866, or thereafter, with no lawful employment or business, or found unlawfully assembling themselves together either in the day- or nighttime, and all white persons so assembling with freedmen, free Negroes, or mulattoes, or usually associating with freedmen, free Negroes, or mulattoes on terms of equality, or living in adultery or fornication with a freedwoman, free Negro, or mulatto, shall be deemed vagrants; and, on conviction thereof, shall be fined in the sum of not exceeding, in the case of a freedman, free Negro, or mulatto, $150, and a white man, $200, and imprisoned at the discretion of the court, the free Negro not exceeding ten days, and the white man not exceeding six months.

Section 5. Be it further enacted, that all fines and forfeitures collected under the provisions of this act shall be paid into the county treasury for general county purposes; and in case any freedman, free Negro, or mulatto shall fail for five days after the imposition of any fine or forfeiture upon him or her for violation of any of the provisions of this act to pay the same, that it shall be, and is hereby made, the duty of the sheriff of the proper county to hire out said freedman, free Negro, or mulatto to any person who will, for the shortest period of service, pay said fine or forfeiture and all costs. This act shall be in force from its passage.

Immediately after this law was passed, Alfred Terry, the commanding general of the U.S. Army in Virginia, forbade its enforcement. He realized the real purpose of the law, regardless of the language to the contrary. His orders had little effect. Vagrancy was enforced and remained on the books into the early 1900s. It was amended over the years, and in 1904, the punishment was reduced to a fine and one year of good behavior.[25]

These laws were ominously similar to those on the books prior to the Civil War that we discussed earlier. Those had required free African Americans to have their registration papers with them at all times or risk imprisonment and hiring out. The practical application of this new law was that one had to stay employed at all times or risk imprisonment and hiring out. African American men were only offered the lowliest jobs and the lowest wages. If they chose not to accept, they could be picked up as vagrants. The law was enforced subjectively and made it very easy for an official to declare somebody a vagrant.[26]

In addition to the Vagrancy Act, the elevation of petty crimes to felonies was another way employed to criminalize African Americans. While the

African American waiters at an outdoor event. *Library of Congress.*

criminal codes did not specifically call out harsher punishments for African Americans, in practice they were more often convicted and penalties were harsher than those for white prisoners.

After the enactment of these laws, prison populations exploded with African Americans. It was then easy to take the next step of promulgating the dogma that they were naturally prone to criminal behavior. This was enthusiastically embraced by the white population. After the passage of the new laws, prison overcrowding became a huge problem. Chain gangs and convict leasing were quickly instituted to reduce the overcrowding, as well as bring in revenue for the commonwealth. The mayor of Richmond had ordered the organization of chain gangs on December 1, 1866. Chain gangs were used for public works such as road building, ditch digging, building repair, land clearing and so on. The chains were to be seven feet long and have a twelve-pound ball attached. They caused painful ulcers and dangerous infections on ankles. Chain gangs were often housed overnight in wagons or crude shelters. The convicts suffered terrible abuses, sometimes ending in

African American men working to pave a road. *Library of Congress.*

death. A sentence of a month on a chain gang might leave one's family destitute, preclude the victim from obtaining employment upon release, cause the loss of living quarters when rent wasn't paid and likely result in hunger and other privations.

Local newspapers faithfully reported arrests and convictions. Three poor souls who were charged with vagrancy were reported in the *Alexandria Gazette* of January 22, 1895:

> *Police Court. Justice Thompson presiding. George Hamilton and George Norton, colored, arrested by officer Griffin, were sent to the chain gang for ninety days as vagrants. John Stevens, colored, arrested by officer Davis, was sent to the chain gang for ninety days as a vagrant.*

Sentences for petty crimes were also reported in the *Daily Dispatch* of February 14, 1868:

Hustings Court of Richmond:
Albert Davis (colored) petit larceny, six months' work in the chain gang.
Lee Thornton (colored) petit larceny, nine months' work in the chain gang.
James Bird (colored), four months' work in the chain gang.
Archer Anderson (colored) misdemeanor, four months' work in the chain gang.

On May 16, 1868, the following appeared in the *Dispatch*:

William Barnes, John White, Henry Smith, Benjamin Harrison, Moses Anderson, George Washington, Daniel Johnson, Simon Loney, Albert Turner, John Anderson, all for petit larceny, all sentenced to the chain gang.

It is notable that the specific crimes for which these people are condemned to the chain gang are not mentioned. It is impossible to know the nature of the crimes or even whether they were actually guilty or just rounded up because labor was needed for the road work.

Other cases gave details about the crime charged. From the *Daily Dispatch* of May 31, 1872:

Lewis Knox (negro) charged with stealing a shovel, valued at two dollars, was sent to the chain gang for thirty days.

The *Daily Dispatch* of March 6, 1868, reported:

CONVICTS RECEIVED: The following convicts were received at the penitentiary yesterday; Abram Wilson (colored), one year for felony, Halifax County. The amount of Wilson's theft was only twelve cents, but he broke a lock to get at it.

What did the Vagrancy Act mean to Emily and her sons? It remained a constant threat to the African American community until 1904. As her boys matured and entered the workforce, this threat hung over them, and every other African American man, as a menacing shadow. In every census record we found, all her sons were gainfully employed, but those records provide only a glimpse every ten years. We don't know what kind of work they were doing in the interim. We know that Walter at one time was an upholsterer, but James and Henry worked various menial jobs throughout their lives. Imagine the feelings if, in between employment, one of her sons was picked up off the street and sent to prison for vagrancy. The little house that David had given to Emily takes on new importance when we think about their situation. One of the definitions of vagrancy was failure to have a verifiable, permanent address. Many newly freed people got caught in that trap, but Emily's sons would not have because of that little house. The two properties David gave her also provided a little (very little) income, and ultimately, as we shall see later, they saved her from destruction.

Property ownership made a tremendous difference to former enslaved people. We have conducted interviews with other African Americans whose ancestors had been given property by their white fathers/former masters after the war, and we have learned how significant that could be. The land gave them independence, food, income and dignity and saved many from the worst abuses and humiliations of the Black codes and later Jim Crow laws. It also provided the second and third generations out of slavery a leg up regarding economic independence.

The intentional criminalization of African Americans has had long-lasting consequences. Before the Civil War, they were criminals if they tried to own themselves. After the Civil War, they were criminalized again. Since the prisons were full of African Americans, it was a short, easy step to characterize them as naturally prone to criminal behavior. The stereotype was created of the ignorant, brutish, dangerous Black man, and it was used to justify every horror to which they were subjected.

As Vladimir Lenin, Adolf Hitler and Joseph Goebbels taught us, if the lie is big enough and repeated often enough, it becomes truth. The pervasiveness of this lie is still apparent today. One has only to look at the way African American men are treated across the criminal justice system.

I can personally relate to this phenomenon. As a young white child living in an all-white neighborhood and going to an all-white school in Northern Virginia, I had virtually no interaction with anybody of any different color. Often, as my family drove along the roads in our station wagon, I noticed the road gangs digging ditches or performing other work along the side of the road. I noticed they were always all "colored." I asked my parents about that. They were not people who encouraged that type of question, so they simply said that if they weren't criminals, they wouldn't be there. Naturally, my parents wouldn't lie to me, so that must be true. I'm sure now that they had grown up being told the same thing and didn't know any better either. Nevertheless, that is what I was taught, and it wasn't until many years later that I learned the truth. I opine that many of the troubles we still have in this country are because most people still have not been enlightened about the Great Lie.

Convict Leasing

Probably the most brutal of all the policies of the criminal justice systems across the South was the convict leasing system. Accounts in history books often give Virginia somewhat of a free ride on this, but convict leasing was certainly used in this state, both to reduce prison overcrowding and to bring in state revenue. In Alabama in 1898, for example, the amount of total state revenue from convict leasing was 73 percent. We were not able to find the number for Virginia. The death rates of leased convicts could be many-fold greater than that of non-leased inmates. Turning again to the *Daily Dispatch* of May 1, 1867, we found the following:

> *NOTICE TO EMPLOYERS:*
> *The General Assembly has passed an act authorizing me, under the direction of the Governor, to employ convicts at the penitentiary at Richmond, or within twenty miles thereof, in improving, repairing, or working on public buildings, grounds and property, or in executing work under contract with individuals or companies. It is provided also that additional shops may be erected by contractors in the penitentiary grounds for the employment of the convicts so hired, at the expense of the contractors.*
>
> *Under the provision of this act there will be a large number of convicts to be hired. I am directed by the governor to direct persons desirous of EMPLOYING CONVICTS to offer PROPOSALS, stating in each case the number of convicts desired, the particular employment in which it is proposed to engage them, and the price per day, week or month offered. It is desirable that proposals be filed with me before the 3rd of May next.*
> *J.F. Pendleton, Superintendent, Penitentiary of Virginia.*

Local newspapers are full of accounts of private individuals who took advantage of this opportunity and hired convicts for things like making shoes, brooms and barrels and other tasks within the penitentiary confines. The convicts also were leased outside the prison walls to railroads, quarries, the James River and Kanawha Canal Company, coal mines and other private businesses.

John Henry

The ballad "John Henry" is the most recorded folk song in American history. The song gives one the impression of a large, strong, independent man who worked on various strenuous jobs and was admired for his great strength. In the brilliantly researched book *Steel Drivin' Man: John Henry*, Scott Reynolds Nelson tells a story much different from the words in that folk song. The song starts out with John Henry being a little baby sitting on the knee of his papa, who picked up a hammer and a piece of steel and said, "Hammer's gonna be the death of me." Nelson states that Henry was actually one of the leased convicts from the Virginia Penitentiary who lost his life working on the Lewis Tunnel in the mountains of Virginia for the Chesapeake and Ohio Railroad.[27]

Nelson tells the story as follows. John Henry was a free African American from Elizabeth City, New Jersey. He was only five feet, one and three-quarters inches tall. At seventeen years of age, he followed the Union army to Virginia during the siege of Petersburg. He was not actually in the army but was probably a paid laborer of some sort. He ended up at City Point, Virginia. City Point had sprung up as the supply depot for Grant at the confluence of the James and Appomattox Rivers and was crowded with ships bringing supplies to the Union army. After the war, it remained a crowded, bustling place. John was caught up in the sweep of arrests that followed passage of the Black codes in April 1866. He was accused of stealing from Wiseman's grocery store. The store carried only items that cost pennies to a few dollars, so it would have been difficult to steal items totaling $20. However, that was the amount he was accused of taking, which elevated the crime to a felony. He was tried and convicted without a jury, sentenced to ten years in the state penitentiary in Richmond, and became prisoner number 467. On December 1, 1868, he was part of a convict labor gang that was leased to the Chesapeake and Ohio Railroad and sent to the mountains to cut the Lewis Tunnel through a mile of solid rock. Conditions for the convicts were terrible, and they were driven hard because the company was up against a deadline. Work in those tunnels was extremely dangerous. Besides the danger of cave-ins, the chipping away of rock by man and machine released microscopic particles of silica dust that settled in the lungs and caused silicosis (inflammation and scarring of the lungs that leads to respiratory insufficiency and death). Over one hundred convicts died working in that tunnel. The state had imposed a fine of $100 for any convict (or his body) that was not returned to Richmond. The reason the

African American men unloading ships at City Point during the siege of Petersburg, Virginia. John Henry worked at City Point prior to his arrest in 1866. *Library of Congress.*

bodies had to be returned was that the railroad had been reporting prisoners who had escaped as dead. John Henry is believed to have been returned to the penitentiary because of illness and to have died there. Hundreds of dead prisoners were buried in a sand pit on the grounds of the penitentiary. The song says John Henry was "taken to the white house" and "buried in the sand." The white house was the penitentiary workhouse, part of the prison complex. The burial ground was hidden from the public until it was accidentally discovered in 1992 during the razing of the old prison complex. Remains of over two hundred bodies, including men, women and children, were found in a sand pit. One of them was probably John Henry. So here was a free man who came to Virginia to work, got caught up in the prison system after passage of the Black codes and was made a slave who met his

State Penitentiary, Richmond, Va.

Virginia State Penitentiary in Richmond, where John Henry was imprisoned, on a 1906 postcard. *Authors' collection.*

death working as a hired convict. From whence came the song? A cook and a water boy who had worked at the camps beside the tunnel had known John Henry and told tales about certain feats of his, and from those, a song was eventually born. John Henry's true story is quite different from the tale told in the children's books and the song we all know. He was another tragic victim of the Black codes.

An article in the *Daily Dispatch* on the morning of April 27, 1871, supports this story. It regarded the governor's visit to the penitentiary:

> *The penitentiary hospital had three or four cases of sickness, and some ten or twelve patients sent from the Chesapeake and Ohio railroad who are suffering chiefly with dropsical affections* [old word for edema, possibly from heart failure], *contracted in the West. The general health of the establishment, however, is excellent, and the whole prison, as far as this penitentiary could be, is in tip top order and as clean as a penny.*

Another article reported that one hundred convicts had been hired out to the railroad.

The Black codes, the chain gangs, the prisons and the convict leasing system were exceptionally successful in keeping the former enslaved—indeed, all

African Americans—at the very bottom of the economic and social hierarchy and afraid to push for their rights guaranteed in the U.S. Constitution. They were intentionally subjugated and only given low-skill, low-paying jobs. An unintended consequence was that the wages of poor whites were also depressed, and the South became locked into an agricultural economy for many years. The result was a depressed, raw materials economy that missed out on the Industrial Revolution and kept both African Americans and whites impoverished. By 1919, the eleven states with the lowest per capita income were all in the South.

Sharecropping

The system of sharecropping was developed across the South to replace the labor formerly provided by enslaved people. Sharecropping initially seemed to be a middle ground between the desire of whites to control the labor force and the desire of African Americans for independence and land. Under sharecropping contracts, families rented land to farm on their own and shared the harvested crops. The tenant had to get his seeds, equipment, mules, food and other supplies from the landowner on credit until the crops came in. The landowner sold the crop and then "divided" the proceeds. The landowner also kept the books. Even if a tenant could read and write and kept his own books, any challenge of the owner's account brought harsh retribution. Most sharecroppers' interviews we have read tell of getting only a few dollars, breaking even or even being in debt to the owner after the tally. Debt precluded them from leaving the property until it was paid, but it was rarely paid under this system. Most people thought they were lucky if they netted a few dollars.

Consider the terms laid out in this contract written in Louisa County, Virginia, in 1866:

> *Articles of agreement between Wm. B. Cooke and his former servants.*
> *In accordance with Gen. Order No. [?], which orders men to make bargains with their former slaves, the following agreement between Wm. B. Cooke on the first part and his former servants, namely Andrew, John, Martha, James for self and children and Caroline for self and her little brother and sister, has been on this day made voluntarily by all parties.*

Young boy from a sharecropper's family working the fields, 1937. *Library of Congress.*

First, the above named servants each and all of them bind themselves to go to work the farm and to do and attend all the business heretofore done by them and to be entirely under the management and control of Wm. B. Cooke to obey punctually all orders given by him and in fact to be and to submit to him as they have ever done heretofore; to finish working and to gather all the crop now on hand, to prepare for a second crop of wheat and winter oats, and to repair fencing and make preparation for another crop, all to be done faithfully and cheerfully.

And Wm. B. Cooke on his part binds himself that if the servants faithfully perform their part of this agreement, that for and on consideration of the same, that he will on the 25th day of December 1865, give to the named servants to be divided amongst them according to their merit and faithfulness in complying with their part of this contract, one fourth of all the corn made on the place this year, one eighth of all the molasses made this year, one half of the wool clipped this year, one half of the cotton raised this year, they shall have the privilege of raising a pig apiece for themselves, the corn to be divided after the hogs are fattened, and that they are to be fed as heretofore until Christmas. The above named articles is to be all that the

Interior of a sharecropper's home, circa 1930. *Library of Congress.*

servants shall in any way clame [sic] *for their services this year, the servants are to clothe themselves out of the said wool or cotton and to pay their own expenses* [illegible] *the servants on their part find themselves that if they or any one of them in any way fail to comply with this agreement and behave disorderly that they shall at once leave the farm and forfeit at once their entire pay and furthermore that if any one or all of them leave here before the 25ᵗʰ of December 1865 without the written consent of Wm. B. Cooke that they at once and forever forfeit all the remuneration herein mentioned, and they further state that, having this agreement read and explained to them by a disinterested party, that they of their own free will and accord willingly assign their names to said agreement in the presents* [sic] *of disinterested witnesses whose names onto this paper as witnesses our hands, this the 15ᵗʰ day of July 1865. Wm. B. Cooke, Andrew X, John X, Martha X, James X, Caroline X. Witness Clarke Goodwin.*[28]

This contract clearly favors Wm. Cooke. It is he who decides if they are cheerful enough, faithful enough or orderly enough. The pay is to be divided among the servants, but who decides who gets what? If, as a group, they receive one-fourth of the corn, that means that each one receives only 5 percent of the corn. And who measures the yields? This contract leaves a lot to be desired, but it still is not as bad as some that were written in the Deep South. The reality of sharecropping for most families meant being tied to the same land they had worked as slaves. They were frequently forbidden to leave until they settled their debt with the landowner, which was almost impossible under the terms of sharecropping. Sharecropping remained the dominant labor system in the South well into the twentieth century.

DOMESTIC WORK

Emily, Maria and Bettie were always listed in census records as domestic workers/servants. There was virtually no employment available to African American women other than domestic work. Both the man and the woman of a household had to work to keep afloat. Emily's situation was even worse, as she was alone. Domestic work was back-breaking, especially for a laundress. Often, white women who had been used to enslaved women obediently obeying every command, no matter how unreasonable, tended to believe they had the right to continue to do so. The women were required to work long hours, often from pre-dawn to after dark. Pay was very low and sometimes nonexistent. If a white family refused to pay wages that were due, the worker usually had no legal recourse. Any questioning of authority was not tolerated. Subservience was demanded.

Domestic workers constantly worried about being raped and/or beaten while at work or on their way to or from their work. Mothers warned daughters entering domestic service to stay out of the white man's way. The rape of Black women by white men was just one more way to let Black men know that they had no power to protect them. Sexual abuse of Black women by white men usually went unpunished. But woe be it to any Black man who raped a white woman or even got caught alone in a room with one. Here is an excerpt from an interview with domestic worker Cleaster Mitchell:

> *I learned very early about abuse from white men when working in people's houses. It was terrible at one time, and these wasn't anybody to tell. Sometimes the wife knew it but she was scared of her husband too. You could go to the wife and she'd say, "Oh just don't pay him no attention," because she would be scared too. He was drunk. Don't pay him no attention. A lot*

Workers at Lexington Laundry in Richmond, Virginia, about 1899. *Library of Congress.*

of people that worked left on that account because you had no alternative. To go to the law didn't mean anything. And I'll tell you, one time in the south it's bad to say, white men are crazy about black women. They would come to your house. They would attack you.[29]

In my own interviews with African Americans from Richmond, they all said that their fathers forbade their daughters from going into domestic service because of the well-known danger of white men. We know that Emily Winfree bore two children after the death of David Winfree. Although Winfree is listed as their father, we know that is not possible, since he was dead. As a domestic servant trying to feed her family, was Emily impregnated by one or more white men? We also know that Maria Winfree bore a son prior to her marriage to John Walker, named Burfoot. At the time, she was a domestic servant working in the house of David Winfree's brother-in-law, Syndenham Walke. He had a son named Burfoot who was almost the same age as Maria. Burfoot is such an unusual name!

The women were humiliated on a daily basis. Also from Cleaster:

> *On Christmas Day, 1936 she* [Cleaster's mother] *was cooking our Christmas dinner and Mr. Roberts came about 10:30 and said to my mother, "Mary, I come after you to go up there to serve for Mrs. Roberts." My mother said, "Well I can't go today because I am preparing my children's Christmas dinner, and I always fix them a Christmas dinner. If I had known, I would have tried to make some kind of arrangements to have gotten started early and maybe I could have served dinner for you all." He was so mad. About an hour later he came back out and called my mother to the car. My mother lived in his house. "I want my house," he said. "I want you to get out of my house, and I want you out of there tomorrow." She just told him, "Yes, sir." After she got through with Christmas dinner, she went down to see Mr. Bennett. He had an old vacant house where the horses and things were stored. That's where we moved, all because she refused, and didn't go because she was cooking our Christmas dinner. That's what you had to contend with. You did what they said or else you suffered the consequence. There was always a repercussion. It was always something.*[30]

Domestic servants often could not enter through the front door. In many cases, they could not use the bathroom in the house. Some had to go home to use the facility and then come back. Some went under the house. They could not eat at the table or even off the plates that their employers used. Their plates were kept separate; in one home, the dog was fed, the plate was washed and then the maid used it. This, in spite of the fact that white children often nursed at the Black nanny's breast.

MILITARY RECONSTRUCTION

As the South had shown convincingly that it could not be trusted to ensure that free men and women were truly free, the Republican-controlled Congress finally had enough. It divided the former Confederacy into five military districts. Virginia became Military District Number One in March 1867. A governor was appointed by General Schofield. Virginia was required to write a new state constitution, which incorporated the Fourteenth Amendment. Military orders were issued that African Americans be registered to vote and also be allowed to run for seats in the constitutional convention, to be held in October 1867. Twenty-four were elected, and with sympathetic white Republican delegates, they had the majority over the Democrats. The resulting constitution had two main important provisions: suffrage for African American men and free public schools (segregated). Finally, things were changing, and some of the rights of citizenship were assured for African Americans. Some even won seats in the Virginia General Assembly in 1871, 1873 and 1875.

The new feeling of hope that resulted from the new constitution was short-lived. Congress had again left a huge loophole. Although the governor was appointed by the military, most public offices were left alone and remained in the hands of former Confederates. In addition, the degree to which the congressional mandates were enforced was entirely dependent on the politics of the current commanding general of the state. Some were sympathetic to the former Rebels. All told, the military did little to intervene in Virginia's business.[31]

DISENFRANCHISEMENT

In spite of the new state constitution, it did not take long for the former Confederates to disenfranchise African Americans through the most creative machinations one might imagine. Some of those are clearly laid out in the book *Race Man* by Ann Alexander.[32] Let us take Richmond as an example. After the Civil War, there were five wards, or voting districts, in Richmond. Each ward had a large contingent of African Americans, but they mostly lived in the northern parts of the wards. New boundary lines were gerrymandered so as to enclose most of the African Americans into a new ward on the north side of the city. This was Jackson Ward, whose boundary was as crooked as a black snake and which had crammed into it twice as many people as there were in some of the wealthy wards. The result of the new ward was to effectively reduce African Americans to a single voting bloc. The upside of this for them was that they were guaranteed at least one seat on city council, and for a while, they were able to exert some influence on Richmond politics. But this wasn't good enough for the whites in control of the city. In 1883, Democrats managed to recapture the General Assembly, and in 1884, they passed the infamous Anderson-McCormick Act, which allowed the Democratic majority to appoint all members of electoral boards in all cities and counties. This act gave partisan (Democratic) workers command and control of voter registration, the conduct of elections and the counting of votes. A period of election fraud was ushered in that was unsurpassed in Virginia's history. The corruption included bribery, fraud, intimidation, stuffing of ballot boxes, destruction of votes, addition of phantom candidates to ballots to spread confusion and intentional delays of voting on election day. In Jackson Ward, for example, with its large majority of African American voters, Black and white voters were put into separate lines and allowed to vote alternately—white, Black, white, Black and so on. When the line of white men had all voted, there was still a long line of Black men waiting. The officials then began to challenge each remaining voter with extensive questions about his registration and residency, even going so far as to make the voter walk with the official to his residence to prove he lived there. All the while, other voters were waiting, and when the polls closed, there were still hundreds of Black men in line who had waited all day but were never allowed to cast their votes.

The corruption allowed—indeed, encouraged—by the Anderson-McCormick Act naturally spilled over and infected the whole state. Eventually, as should have been expected, the fraud became so rampant and widespread that even Democratic candidates were "out-frauding" one another. Clearly, they had to figure out a different, legal way to keep African Americans from voting. But how? The Democrats pushed through a referendum calling for a new constitution by promising electoral reform and better state government.

On February 16, 1901, the General Assembly passed an act calling for the election of delegates to serve in Virginia's fifth constitutional convention. On June 12, 1901, one hundred delegates (eighty-eight Democrats and twelve Republicans) assembled in the old hall of the House of Delegates at the capitol. The main question for the delegates was how to legally get around the Fourteenth Amendment and eliminate the African American vote. John Mitchell, the editor of the African American *Richmond Planet*, accused them of a "plan to violate the U.S. Constitution without violating the U.S. Constitution."[33] Their solution follows:

> *Section 19. There shall be general registrations in the counties, cities and towns of the State during the years nineteen hundred and two and nineteen hundred and three at such times and in such manner as may be prescribed by an ordinance of this convention. At such registrations, every male citizen of the United States having the qualifications of age and residence required in Section 18 shall be entitled to register if he be:*
> *First: A person who, prior to the adoption of this Constitution, served in time of war in the Army or Navy of the United States, of the Confederate States, or of any State of the United States or of Confederate States: or*

Second: A son of any such person: or,

Third: A person who owns property, upon which, for the year next preceding that in which he offers to register, state taxes aggregating at least one dollar have been paid: or

Fourth: A person able to read any section of this constitution submitted to him by the officers of the registration and to give a reasonable explanation of the same; or, if unable to read such section, able to understand and give a reasonable explanation thereof when read to him by the officers.

Section 20. after the first day of January, nineteen hundred and four, every male citizen of the United States, having the qualifications of age and residence required in Section 18, shall be entitled to register, provided:

First, that he has personally paid to the proper officer all state poll taxes assessed or assessable against him, under this or the former Constitution, for the three years next preceding that in which he offers to register: or, if he come of age at such time that no poll tax shall have been assessable against him for the year preceding the year in which he offers to register, has paid one dollar and fifty cents, in satisfaction of the first year's poll tax assessable against him, and:

Second: That, unless physically unable, he make application to register in his own handwriting, without aid, suggestion, or memorandum in the presence of the registration officers, stating therein his name, age, date and place of birth, residence and occupation at the time and for the two years next preceding, and whether he has previously voted, and, if so, the state, county, and precinct in which he voted last, and:

Third: That he answer on oath any and all questions affecting his qualifications as an elector submitted to him by the officers of registration, which questions, and his answers thereto, shall be reduced to writing, certified by the said officers, and preserved as a part of their official records.

Normally, a new state constitution would need to be ratified by the voters, and the General Assembly had planned to do that, prior to the convention. Later, they realized that voters who were about to be disenfranchised would not vote for ratification, so the convention instead announced the new constitution by proclamation, and it became law on July 10, 1902. The old poll books were purged, and all voters were required to register (or try to register) afresh. Both the poll tax and the literacy requirements remained in effect in Virginia until they were overturned by the federal courts and Congress in the 1960s.

The African American community across Virginia rose up to challenge the new constitution. They raised money for a lawyer, James H. Hayes, to take up the cause in the federal court system. After losing at the circuit court level, he appealed all the way to the Supreme Court, which dismissed the case in April 1904.[34]

That was the end of the era in Virginia during which African American men voted. The next two to three generations never got a chance. Outcomes of elections were determined before voting occurred, so few people, white or Black, even went to the polls.

The push to eliminate the African American vote in Virginia was mirrored in other southern states. After similar actions in other states, literacy tests sprang up throughout the South. Virginia's version was an "understanding clause," which gave officials broad discretion as to the questions they asked potential registrants. On September 13, 1902, the registrar in Warren County, Virginia, asked Charles Wilson Butler, an African American blacksmith, to explain section 4 of the new state constitution. Butler replied that "you men have no right to refuse to register me." But the registrar wrote that Butler was "not admitted."[35] Here is the section of the Virginia Constitution that Butler was asked to explain:

> *That no man, or set of men, is entitled to exclusive or separate emoluments or privileges from the community, but in consideration of public services; which not being descendible, neither ought the offices of magistrate, legislator or judge be hereditary.*

The new constitution had the desired effect. For example, in the city of Richmond, the number of registered Black voters prior to the convention was 6,407. After the convention, it was reduced to 760. An unintended consequence was that poor, illiterate white men were also disenfranchised if they were not veterans. Finally, the old Rebels had their way. They had created an all-white, one-party government that maintained control of Virginia until the middle of the twentieth century.

Let us pause to remember that Emily and her family lived in the midst of all of this. Were her sons and sons-in-law some of those men who stood in line on election day, waiting until all the white men had voted and then still standing there when the polls closed? How many times would a man be willing to do that? After the 1902 constitution, did they try to re-register? Like others we know of, did they study in preparation for the questions they would be asked, only to be embarrassed and belittled? We know that many men stayed away, unwilling to be humiliated again and again. We have talked about the desperate economic situation of the Winfree family. It is unlikely that they would have had the money to pay the poll taxes even if they could make it past the literacy tests. What was it like to be a grown man with so little control of his surroundings? All of Emily's sons had passed on long before the Voting Rights Act of 1965. They most likely went their whole lives without exercising their constitutionally guaranteed right to vote. The grandsons probably had little chance of voting either. It is likely that Emily's great-grandchildren (men and women) were the first in the family who were allowed to vote in Virginia.

COMPLICITY OF THE SUPREME COURT

We now must return to 1875 and talk about the Supreme Court's complicity in the subjugation of African Americans. Congress, distressed by the continued recalcitrance of the South, made another attempt. Still controlled by the Republicans who were trying to reform the South (known as Radical Republicans), Congress passed the Civil Rights Act of 1875. The Fourteenth Amendment had been written too broadly. The new law laid out specifically what civil rights were guaranteed, as well as the penalties for anybody who would deny others the rights of citizenship. Very, very importantly, it transferred jurisdiction away from the states' judicial systems to the federal judicial system. It even gave federal authorities the power to arrest state officials. This reignited a firestorm that was similar to the one that had led to the Civil War and the one that is still with us today. It pitted states' rights advocates, who thought they had the right to treat the people they used to own in any way they chose, against a federal government that was trying to ensure the United States Constitution applied equally to all American citizens.

The Radical Republicans who had pushed the equal rights legislative agenda were losing their majority in both chambers of Congress. Their time was coming to a close, but they had done their job. Now it was up to the United States Judiciary to uphold the constitutional amendments that had been ratified by the country. The Supreme Court, to which former slave owners were appointed, failed miserably. The only way to describe the rulings of the justices of the Supreme Court between 1865 and 1903 was a complete betrayal of African Americans. They essentially ruled in a long series of cases that the

Fourteenth Amendment was unconstitutional. This thinking defied reason, because how can something that is in the Constitution be unconstitutional? With each ruling, the world of African Americans shrank.

A quote by Lawrence Goldstein in his brilliant book *Inherently Unequal* summarizes the role of the court in the denial of rights for African Americans:

> *With three constitutional amendments and myriad enforcement acts on the books, after the unstinting efforts of leaders in the Congress, after the impeachment in 1868 of a president who attempted to subvert equal rights for emancipated slaves, by the dawn of the twentieth century the United States had become a nation of Jim Crow laws, quasi-slavery, and precisely the same two-tiered system of justice that had existed in the slave era. Throughout the South, black Americans could not go to school with whites, could not ride next to them in streetcars, sit next to them in theatres or restaurants, could not be buried in the same cemeteries, could not use the same public toilets; black Americans were denied the right to vote, to sit on juries, and often were denied the right to have a trial at all. The descent of the United States into enforced segregation, into a nation where human beings could be tortured and horribly murdered without trial, is a story profoundly tragic and profoundly American. Over nearly three decades, the Supreme Court was a central player in this tale.*[36]

One of the early key cases was *United States v. Cruikshank*, a case out of Colfax, Louisiana. Republicans had won the governor's race of 1872. The Republican Party in the South was the one whose members believed in equal rights for African Americans. This win angered the Democrats, who did not want those rights honored. A white mob stormed the Colfax courthouse, which was guarded by African American members of the official Louisiana militia. Badly outnumbered, the militia surrendered and gave up their arms, but the mob slaughtered them anyway. Over one hundred were shot, even as they tried to flee, and others were burned when the mob set the courthouse on fire. Three white people were also killed. President Grant had to send in troops to restore order. United States attorney J.R. Beckworth charged almost one hundred members of the mob. Three were convicted, but they appealed all the way to the Supreme Court, arguing that the state, not the federal government, had jurisdiction in the matter. The court agreed and overturned the convictions on March 27, 1876. This decision signaled that the judicial branch of the federal government of the United States refused to enforce the Fourteenth Amendment of the Constitution or the Civil Rights

Act of 1875. Thus, the court had removed any barrier to the South's passing of law after law to ensure the white domination of African Americans. Knowing the court's position, federal prosecutors did not bother to bring forward very many cases, knowing that outcomes were predetermined, so there was little done to enforce the law.[37]

Rutherford B. Hayes's Back-Door Deal

In 1876, the situation in the South continued to deteriorate for African Americans. Violence against them was rising, even with the military presence, and it was clear that more troops would be needed. But by now, northerners were tiring of dealing with their southern brethren, and Congress was more and more reluctant to fund the troops. It seemed that Lincoln's great ambition of healing the nation was just too much trouble. The southern states had reentered the Union—some maintained that they had never actually left—and they weren't threatening to secede again. So if they thought they should be allowed to denigrate, imprison and massacre their "Negroes" as they pleased, why should the rest of the country interfere? The Supreme Court had made it clear that it would not. Then came the final blow: a presidential election between Democrat Samuel J. Tilden and Republican Rutherford B. Hayes, who had previously supported the attempts by Congress to ensure equal rights for African Americans. After the election, the electoral vote count was very close and ultimately depended on the votes in Louisiana, Florida and South Carolina. While Congress was struggling to figure out how to certify a winner, an unwritten, back-door compromise was made in which the southern Democrats agreed to give Hayes their electoral votes and promised to honor the rights of African Americans in exchange for removal of all federal troops from their states.[38] Hayes became president, and one of his first acts was to order the removal of federal troops from the South. The promise made by the southern Democrats proved to be empty. And that was the end of Reconstruction. The Republicans who had tried to cleanse the South of the stain of slavery gave up. The South systematically entrapped its African American citizens with a series of new Jim Crow laws, intimidation, fraud, lynching, gerrymandering, disenfranchisement and any other means it could devise. Meanwhile, the Supreme Court continued to issue a series of decisions that absolved the federal government from responsibility in enforcing federal law.

SUPREME COURT LEGALIZES SEGREGATION

The Supreme Court decision that clinched legal segregation was *Plessy v. Ferguson*, in 1892. Homer Plessy was an African American who was arrested for refusing to move from his first-class seat to the Jim Crow car on the East Louisiana Railroad. His case wound its way up to the Supreme Court. The defense erred by not bringing up the fact that the Jim Crow car was far inferior to the first-class, all-white car. On May 18, 1896, by a 7–1 majority, the Supreme Court ruled against Plessy.[39] The majority opinion stated that separation of races was not discriminatory because it applied equally to both white and Black citizens. Thus was born the doctrine of "separate but equal." This ruling had a profound effect on the nation. It led to the most stringent segregation laws. African American passengers were forced to sit at the back of streetcars or stand if there were not enough seats for whites. They were made to sit in separate sections of theaters, libraries and train stations. People of color could not use water fountains, bathrooms, beaches or swimming pools used by whites. They could only order takeout food from restaurants that served whites. African American children attended separate, usually ramshackle schools. Social activities, along with everything from sports teams to funeral parlors, were segregated. When African Americans donated blood, it was segregated from that of white donors. Later on, the court denied cases that challenged discriminatory restrictions on voter registration that had been written into new state constitutions, not just in Virginia but all over the South.[40] It wasn't until the famous *Brown v. Board of Education* ruling that the concept of separate but equal was struck down. But that was fifty-eight years later—too late for millions.

Segregation laws were not just suggestions. Violators were treated severely by the law, as well as by terrorist enforcers. As docents at the Virginia Museum of History and Culture, we encounter visitors from all over the country. One afternoon, an elderly African American matron from New York was touring the museum, and we were discussing segregation. She related the following story. As a child growing up in New York, she did not know about segregated bathrooms, drinking fountains and such. One summer, she came down to Richmond to spend time with her aunt, her mother's sister. They were out and about when she needed to relieve herself. Not noticing the whites-only and colored-only signs, she innocently walked right into the whites-only ladies' room. She said her aunt ran in there, grabbed her by the arm and dragged her all the way down the street, then shrieked at her, blurting out,

"What are you trying to do? Get us killed!" The poor girl didn't know what she had done. That evening, her aunt called her mother and told her she must come get her and take her back to New York because she didn't know how to act down here. What a lovely visit! As an older woman, she still remembers this painful incident.

LYNCHING

Segregation was enforced by any means necessary, but the most terrifying of these was lynching. This was controlled to some extent until Hayes pulled out the federal troops, after which violence escalated. "Lynch law" took over by 1880. Lynchings often involved ritual torture and burning of the bodies and often included participation of local authorities.[41]

In 1892, an African American man was lynched in Providence Forge, Virginia. The act was admiringly described in the *Richmond Dispatch* and followed several days later by an opinion piece that further justified the act. From the *Richmond Dispatch* of April 9, 1892:

HUNG IN THE COURT-HOUSE YARD:
The Merited Fate of Isaac Brandon, the Charles City fiend.
Providence Forge, April 8. A body of seventy-five or eighty masked men, about 11:00 Wednesday night, took Isaac Brandon, the Negro who was in jail at Charles City Courthouse charged with assault upon a young lady, from the jail and hung him from a tree in the court-house yard. They surrounded the house of the sheriff while they broke into the jail. Sheriff Nance woke up and came out, when he was ordered to go back, which he refused to do, and after a few moments they left, but the deed had been very quietly done. An experienced locksmith must have opened the door, as it was double-locked and the locks very strong. A little son of the Negro was staying with him. The boy said that the men entered the jail with pistols in hand and told Brandon to cross his hands behind him. He asked them if they were going to hang him. They told him that they were. He said, "Well you are going to hang an innocent man." Whether he confessed afterwards of course is not known. His body was found hanging the next morning. No person here doubts his guilt. The lynching was very thoroughly and strictly arranged, and no one has the least idea where it started or who the parties were.

Thirteen days later, on April 22, this opinion piece appeared in the *Richmond Dispatch*:

> *HOW TO STOP SOUTHERN OUTRAGES*
> *A delegation of Negroes yesterday waited on the President* [that would have been Harrison] *and induced him to listen to their tale of woe about "southern outrages." In view of the approaching campaign, he gave them what comfort he could, which was necessarily scant. Among other things he advised them to collect and publish the statistics. When this tabulation is made it will be seen that nearly all the "outrages" spring from two classes of crimes that the blacks are in the habit of committing. One of these is cold blooded murder: the other, and the most frequent, is worse than murder. The negroes can achieve a cessation of the "outrages" against which they murmur by ceasing to commit these crimes. In no other possible way can they accomplish what they wish. Stop these crimes and the "outrages" will stop themselves. Hundreds of times we have seen in print in negro papers, bitter denunciations of the southern people for the swiftness with which they lynch black fiends, but never once have we seen the negros advised to shake off their lustful instincts. If punishment were less speedy and certain than it now is, unprotected women in lonely country places could not feel safe for a moment.*

On April 7, 2019, the Virginia Department of Historic Resources placed the first historical marker to highlight a Virginia lynching, describing what happened to Mr. Brandon. It is on the Virginia Capitol Trail near the Charles City Courthouse.

In some cases, lynchings were advertised beforehand. They occurred as a result of a crime, perceived crime or racially charged incident. Lynchings were less numerous in Virginia than in the Deep South, but there were around seventy-six during this era. They were very rarely prosecuted. Many lynchings involved accusations of violation of a white woman by a Black man. The white population promulgated the lie that Black men were strangely allured by white women and couldn't keep their hands off them. It is absurd that this lie was believed, given the number of enslaved women who were raped by white masters. Further, during the Civil War, most documented accounts of rape by Union soldiers were of African American women. One soldier wrote home that it "seems to be their object to commit rape on every Negro woman they can find."[42] In reality, African American women were much more likely to be raped by white men than the opposite.

One reason that there were fewer lynchings in Virginia than in other southern states was that the state government wanted to protect its reputation as an orderly state. State officials sometimes sent troops to protect potential lynching victims. Rather than allow "lynch law," the state used the courts to maintain the racial hierarchy. They quite readily convicted and executed African Americans. The sentence for an African American man convicted of raping a white woman was death. Here are some other examples. A white woman stole a cow in Henrico County (second offense) and was sentenced to one month in jail and fined $5.00. An African American man stole a calf and was sentenced to five years in the penitentiary. A white man in East Radford was convicted of killing an African American man and fined $10.00. An African American man robbed a white man and was hanged.

In the case of Richard Brown (an African American who drove a delivery cart for Charles H. Page, a coal merchant), Page was fined $2.00 by the city for operating the cart without a license, and he deducted the $2.00 from Brown's $3.33 weekly wages. Brown protested, saying it was not his fault that the owner had not paid the fee and he couldn't take care of his family on $1.33. He threatened to take the money. Page returned the $2.00, and Brown went home to his family. The next day, he was arrested on the charge of highway robbery, quickly found guilty and sentenced to five years in the state penitentiary. John Mitchell, known as the fighting editor of the African American newspaper the *Richmond Planet*, took up Brown's cause. Mitchell managed to get the judge to reduce the charge to assault and battery and the sentence reduced to one year. Since no assault or battery had actually occurred, Mitchell was not satisfied. He appealed to Governor O'Farrell to pardon Brown. Finally, Mitchell convinced Page to say the "boy" had learned his lesson, and he would not object if he was pardoned, so the governor signed the order.[43] Outrageous cases such as these were commonplace in Richmond. One false move, one failure to be subservient, could land a person in jail, destroy his family and possibly end up with his death. Richard Brown was lucky that John Mitchell was there to notice his case and help him, but what about the thousands of victims who did not catch the eye of somebody willing to fight for them? Stories like these in Virginia and the South could fill several books.

One Drop of Colored Blood

One could not enforce segregation laws if one could not tell who was "Negro," who was Indian and who was white. There had been so many children who had been born from parents who were different colors. Some of them were "passing" as white when they actually had "Negro" ancestors. The state wanted to be sure, so in 1924, Virginia passed the Racial Integrity Act. Key provisions are stated below:

> *Be it enacted by the General Assembly of Virginia, That the State Registrar of Vital Statistics may as soon as practicable after the taking effect of this act, prepare a form whereon the racial composition of any individual, as Caucasian, negro, Mongolian, American Indian, Asiatic Indian, Malay, or any mixture thereof, or any other non-Caucasic strains, and if there be any mixture, then the racial composition of the parents and other ancestors, in so far as ascertainable, so as to show in what generation such mixture occurred, may be certified by such individual, which form shall be known as a registration certificate....*
>
> *It shall be a felony for any person wilfully or knowingly to make a registration certificate false as to color or race. The wilful making of a false registration or birth certificate shall be punished by confinement in the penitentiary for one year.*
>
> *No marriage license shall be granted until the clerk or deputy clerk has reasonable assurance that the statements as to color of both man and woman are correct.*
>
> *If there is reasonable cause to disbelieve that applicants are of pure white race, when that fact is stated, the clerk or deputy clerk shall withhold the granting of the license until satisfactory proof is produced that both applicants are "white persons" as provided for in this act. The clerk or deputy clerk shall use the same care to assure himself that both applicants are colored, when that fact is claimed.*
>
> *5. It shall hereafter be unlawful for any white person in this State to marry any save a white person, or a person with no other admixture of blood than white and American Indian. For the purpose of this act, the term "white person" shall apply only to the person who has no trace whatsoever of any blood other than Caucasian; but persons who have one-sixteenth or less of the blood of the American Indian and have no other non-Caucasic blood shall be deemed to be white persons. All laws heretofore passed and now in effect regarding the intermarriage of white and colored persons shall apply to marriages prohibited by this act.*

The reason white people who had only one-sixteenth of American Indian blood could still be called white was because so many white elitists proudly claimed to be descendants of Pocahontas. This became known as the "Pocahontas Exception." Today, there are an estimated 100,000 such claimants. The Racial Integrity Act was overturned in 1967 by the Warren Supreme Court.[44]

LEAVING: THE GREAT MIGRATION

By the early 1900s, many African American people in the South had had enough, and World War I offered them a way out. The war effort required a huge influx of industrial workers to the North, and southern African Americans were recruited, sometimes with offers of pay that was three times what they could get in southern states, as well as free transportation. Between then and the 1970s, six million people migrated to the North, where they could become something other than a lowest-level citizen and also participate in democracy. Most of those from Virginia went to Washington, D.C., Baltimore, Philadelphia, New York and Boston. This migration left the South with a dearth of laborers, and some authorities tried to halt the exit by arresting them on railroad platforms on grounds of vagrancy or even tearing up their tickets. Some people escaped in coffins or traveled to a town where they weren't known in order to board the train.[45]

The details of a train trip between Virginia and New York serve to illustrate how insane the segregation laws were. There were lighted signs in all the cars that said "white only" and "colored only." If a colored person boarded in Virginia, for example, the law said he must ride in the Jim Crow car. It was always the first one after the engine. A trip in that car guaranteed one would be covered with coal dust and smoky ashes as the train chugged along. As soon as the train pulled into Washington, D.C., which was the gateway to desegregation, the lights in the signs were turned off and the colored people were allowed to pick up their belongings and go sit anywhere they chose. On return trips, the lights would go back on in D.C., and everybody had to scramble to move from their chosen seats back to the Jim Crow car. After "separate but equal" was finally struck down by the Warren court, some conductors still insisted on segregating their passengers, many of whom would be so confused and intimidated that they would just stay in the Jim Crow car the whole trip.[46]

The migrants' new lives were not without troubles and racism. In big cities like Chicago, Eastern European immigrants had arrived first and resented the new migrants. They competed for jobs and housing. The whites violently defended the racial purity of their neighborhoods, effectively blocking African American families from getting out of the overcrowded ghettos. As more and more people arrived from the South, they were crammed into a small area on the south side of the city. Landlords took advantage of them and did little to maintain the dwellings while charging rents that could be 50 percent higher than what whites paid for similar accommodations. And just like in the land from which they had fled, the migrants ended up doing the most menial jobs.[47]

In spite of all this, people continued to come, and most did not return to the South. They persevered because they felt free. Urban Black districts and Black culture arose in places like Harlem, and the artistic movement known as the Harlem Renaissance came about. Although true integration was never achieved, a Black middle class started to form that included people like Thurgood Marshall and Langston Hughes. People started thinking about civil rights issues. The next generations had greater chances for advancement, although some fell behind. In later years, as the South opened up, new generations returned to their "homeland" and took northern ideas and opinions with them. This accelerated change in the South.

One of the migrants was a poor five-year-old boy from Mississippi. He was taken from his mother in Mississippi to live with his grandfather on his farm in Michigan. His grandfather had been so desperate to leave the South that he had bought the farm sight unseen and left. The little boy was so traumatized by the move that he developed a severe stutter. He tells how he was mocked and ridiculed by the children in Sunday school about it. He was so embarrassed that he just stopped talking. He was almost mute for eight years, talking only to the animals on the farm. When he finally entered high school, a teacher took him under his wing and encouraged him to read his original poetry aloud to his class. When he did that, he didn't stutter. With the teacher's help, the boy eventually overcame his problem, and most would agree he led a pretty successful life. His name was James Earl Jones, and he has related this story in several interviews.

Bill Russell migrated as a child from Louisiana; John Coltrane came from South Carolina. Diana Ross's parents went north from Virginia, and Toni Morrison's came from Alabama. One must wonder if these and others like them would have prospered as they did, had they or their families remained in the South.

Chapter 9

EMILY'S POSTWAR YEARS

Now that we have some understanding of the years between the Civil War and the civil rights era, let us continue the story of Emily and her family. Here she was, with five children and no other adult to help. How was she to care for these children whom she was so determined to keep together? One thing she did was apply for rations from the Freedman's Bureau, set up by Congress to assist newly freed persons.

Emily also tried to utilize the properties. Five months after David's death, Emily's trustee petitioned the Chesterfield County court to grant her permission to cut timber off the 109.5-acre tract in Chesterfield County to build a comfortable house (Appendix III). He cited her five children and her only income being rent from the house in Manchester. As we shall discuss later, there were actually two structures on her place in Manchester. She rented one of them out and lived in the other. Her house was 476 square feet. The court agreed to her plan. We know from later documents that a house was, in fact, built on the property and that she did move to Chesterfield County. When she again applied for rations from the Freedman's Bureau in 1868, she was "living in the country." She was also listed as sick and very destitute.

The move to Chesterfield allowed her to increase her rent income from the Manchester property. Apparently, though, the move didn't work out for her, because the 1870 census places her back in Manchester. Perhaps it was too hard to find work in the country. Perhaps, if she was sick, she needed to be close to a physician. Whatever the cause, she moved back into the little

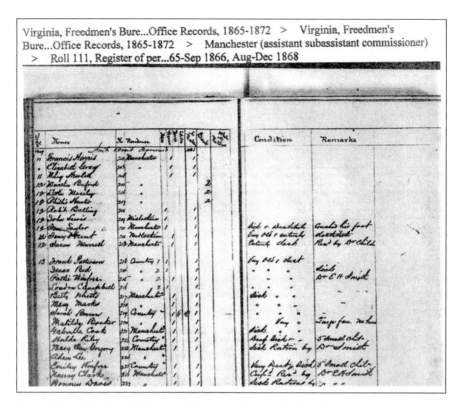

A page from a Freedman's Bureau rations book showing Emily as living in the country, sick, destitute and with five small children. *Freedman's Bureau Records.*

house in Manchester. Maria was fourteen now and was at home tending to Bettie, age eleven; Walter, age eight; James, age five; and Henry, age four. There was also a new baby, Clifford, we believe born sometime in 1869. We have not found his father, but it could not have been David, who had been dead for two years. I suppose it is possible that the census taker mistook a two-year-old for a one-year-old if he was small. We know the census takers made many errors. If David was not the father, it is possible that Emily, as a domestic worker, had been raped, with Clifford being the result. When Clifford died years later, David was listed as his father, but that is another question that remains unanswered.

The census records we examined for Emily's neighborhood in Manchester show the jobs that African Americans held. Virtually every female was a servant or domestic worker. Men were day laborers (most of them), cotton factory workers, tobacco factory workers and firemen on the railroads. All of these were menial jobs.

"AUNT" EMILY

For the past thirty three years the cook for the Lodge has been Emily Winfree, known to all of the Craftsmen as "Aunt Emily." Numerous opossums have "Aunt" Emily prepared for the Lodge on the celebrations of the festivals of the two Saints John. She is a polite mulatto, an efficient cook, and has prepared many splendid suppers during the long years in which she has been engaged by the Lodge. On 'Possum Night (St. John the Evangelist) "Aunt" Emily is always at her best. In this connection it may be appropriate to add that the night of St. John the Evangelist has been known as 'Possum Night for many, many years. This is one of the most interesting traditions of the Lodge, and it deserves to be written up and spread upon the records.

A page in a history of Manchester Lodge, devoted to "Aunt Emily." *Manchester Lodge #14 A.F. and A.M.*

We have two artifacts from Emily's employment. The Masonic Manchester Lodge #14 employed her for thirty-three years to prepare meals for meetings and events. The lodge members thought enough of "Aunt Emily" to dedicate a full page to her in the book they published in 1906.[48] David Winfree's brother-in-law William T. Lithgow may have played a role in getting Emily that job. He was married to David's sister Martha Elizabeth and was the

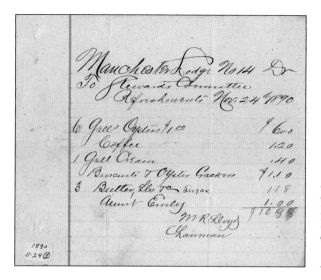

An account of banquet expenses at Manchester Lodge showing "Aunt Emily" was paid one dollar on November 24, 1890. *Virginia Museum of History and Culture.*

tyler for the lodge for many years. The tyler was charged with examining the Masonic credentials of anyone wishing to enter the lodge and admitting only those qualified to attend the current business.

Emily is referred to as "Aunt Emily," a polite mulatto—not Mrs. Winfree. The lodge members obviously thought highly of Emily. After all, they devoted a whole page to her. It just never occurred to them to respect her. We asked current lodge members if this could have been a full-time job, but they said she would have only been hired on the occasions when they had an event. We also found a receipt for one dollar to "Aunt Emily," who had prepared dinner for a lodge meeting on November 14, 1890.

Let us take a moment to think about the use of the term "Aunt Emily" rather than Mrs. Winfree. We often see terms like this used for African Americans, even many years after the Civil War. Take Uncle Remus, Uncle Ben and Aunt Jemima as examples. Those usages perhaps were meant affectionately, but they were, in fact, demeaning. Some white owners talked about their enslaved people being a part of the family and professed to care lovingly for them. Even after emancipation, white housewives who employed African American maids talked about the close bond between them and their help. But interviews with the housewives revealed they actually knew very little about the lives their help lived or even where they lived. They did not wonder who took care of their maids' children while their mothers were cooking, cleaning and being nursemaid for white children until after dark. Many white women expressed hurtful feelings when they saw their maids years later, outside of work, and were not received warmly. They wondered

Manchester Lodge #14 at Fifth and Porter Streets in Manchester, a few blocks from Emily's home. The lodge is now demolished. *Benjamin B. Weisiger III.*

why they were not greeted with open arms.[49] What they never realized was the mask that these employees were forced to wear in the presence of white people—the need to constantly stay subservient, obedient and cheerful, never daring to complain or voice an opinion. They never thought to find out who was behind the mask. That thoughtless ignorance is the very definition of "white privilege." It pervades our society still today.

Emily certainly must have worked multiple jobs to support her family, but we have found no records other than from the lodge. Emily's sons don't appear to have ever worked on farms or plantations. They worked as laborers, cooks, drivers and so on. Walter became an upholsterer, and Clifford became a schoolteacher.

After the 1870 census, there are no records of Emily or her family for the next ten years. We find them again in the 1880 census. Maria had married John H. Walker in 1878 and moved out of the house. Emily was still working as a servant, but now the children were contributing. Bettie, twenty-one, was a servant also. Walter, eighteen, was a driver. James, fifteen, was also working, but his occupation is illegible. Henry was "at school." All were still living in the cottage in Manchester except Clifford, ten, who was living down the street with neighbors; or at least that's where he was when the census taker came around. We have taken the liberty of imagining a conversation among them.

The four of them wearily made their various ways back to the cottage. Emily and Bettie didn't have far to go. They had spent the day delivering the freshly washed, dried and ironed laundry to several of the white houses in the neighborhood. Back and forth they went all day, delivering clean laundry and picking up dirty to tote home and start all over again. Their best customer was David Winfree's sister, Mrs. Walke. She lived just two blocks away and always paid them a little extra. The work was pure drudgery. They had to start a fire out back so they could boil a huge tub of water, scrub all the clothes with lye soap, change the water to rinse, wring them out and hang them out to dry. Then they started all over again. After drying, the laundry was taken inside, and a cast iron was heated atop the stove and all the clothes were carefully ironed. This was their life, day after day.

Henry was at the cottage already. When he got home from school, he did his lessons and then his chores around the house while his mama and sister came and went with the laundry. Always the lessons came first, though. His mother was very strict about that. She knew he would only get a few years of schooling, and she wanted him to get the most out of them that he could.

Emily and Bettie got cleaned up so they could start dinner. Emily had cooked a big dinner at the Possum lodge for the previous evening's meeting, and they had let her bring home some leftovers, so they would be eating high on the hog tonight—seven pieces of fried chicken, a big bowl of potato salad and green beans cooked with fatback. And they were hoping Walter would bring something extra. He drove a truck for a produce company, and most times when a box of fruit or vegetables started to go bad, Mr. Stoddard would let him bring it home. Sure enough, today he showed up with a big box of apples, so Bettie started to peel them right away.

James was the last to get home. He was only fifteen, but it had been necessary for him to give up his schooling to help out. He had a job sweeping up in the hardware store downtown. It didn't offer any chance of extra food, but at least it brought in a little much-needed money.

They warmed up the chicken and beans, and the family sat down at the tiny table. "Lordy, my back is so tired from toting that laundry today I can't wait to get on my mattress tonight," said Emily. "That's all right, Mama, I'll rub some witch hazel on it after dinner and you can rest while I clean up," said Bettie. "That sounds wonderful, child. Henry, are all your lessons done?" "Yes, Ma'am." "And what did you learn in school today?" "We learned about when Thomas Jefferson wrote the Declaration of Independence." "Oh, you mean the one that says all men are created equal," Walter interjected. "Yeah," said Henry.

"Boy, don't you know anything about—" "Now hush up, Walter," said Emily. "Leave the boy alone and let's have a quiet dinner." "OK, Mama, but he needs to know."

Emily constantly worried about Walter. He got riled up so easily and didn't know how to hold his tongue. One day he was gonna mouth off to the wrong white man, and the next thing he would be on a chain gang, working on the canal. Lots of people die on them chain gangs. He was just so angry, and no matter how many times she told him that's just the way it's gotta be for now, he couldn't seem to make peace with it. She took him to church every week, but it didn't help. She just wished he could get out of here somehow and go up north.

"What's wrong with your face, James? You have a big bruise." "Nothing, Mama." "Don't tell me nothing, tell me what happened." "Well, after I swept up this morning, a man came in and saw me standing there and asked me where the bow saws were. I'm not supposed to wait on the customers, so I started to go get Mr. Donavan. The man said, 'Don't you ignore me, boy, I asked you where the bow saws were.' I tried to tell him I was getting Mr. Donavan from the back, but he punched me in the face, and I went crashing into the nail bin. Nails went flying all over the floor. Mr. Donavan heard that, and he came out and started to holler at me until he saw the customer. He got the bow saw for him, and after, when I told him what happened, he said, 'That's OK, boy. Just clean up the nails and go on with your business.'" "I'll go down there and give him some business," said Walter. "You'll do no such thing. Do you want to get yourself killed? There was another lynching just twenty miles south of here last week. James just has to learn to take it. I don't want to have to send him away in the middle of the night, like Mr. Jones did with his boy, and never see him again."

"Mama, I have something to tell you," said Bettie. "You know that Mr. Merrifield who came over here the other night to see me?" "You mean that white boy?" said Walter. "Well, he asked me to marry him." There was stunned silence at the table. Emily slowly put down her fork and fixed her gaze on Bettie. "You know what happens to colored girls that get mixed up with white boys, don't you? You know very well what happened to Grandma and to me and to Maria." "I know, Mama, but that wouldn't happen if nobody knew I was colored. He wants me to marry him and go back to Rhode Island with him, so nobody would know. I'm so light I could pass. Our daddy was white. That means I'm half white and half colored, so I figure I have the right to choose. I choose white. I love Mr. Merrifield, and I'm so tired of being colored. Up north, if I was white, I wouldn't have to do other folks' laundry for the rest of my life. I would do my own laundry and clean my own house and raise my own babies. Maybe I could even get an office job or something." "You would be denying your family, daughter." "No I wouldn't. I'll come back to see you, I promise." Emily looked at Bettie for a long time. Finally, with a tear running down her cheek, she stood and said, "And what will you tell your children about us?" and went outside. The conversation ended, but they all knew it would come up again.

Chapter 10

SICKNESS STRIKES

During Emily's time, there were no social safety nets like social security, unemployment insurance or Medicaid. For a family existing on the edge, there was no room for error or extra misfortune. But that is what happened to the Winfrees. From October 1885 until November 1886, a period of thirteen months, Emily and most of her family became very ill and were treated by Dr. S.L. Ingram, a white physician who lived a few blocks away. According to Dr. Ingram's report, Emily was the most severely ill. This protracted illness most certainly severely reduced or eliminated the household income, and the family became even more destitute. She did not even have the money to pay Ingram the thirty-six dollars she owed him. We do not know the cause of their illness. Death reports in the local papers mention all sorts of demises, but the two that showed up most frequently were diphtheria and consumption (tuberculosis). Scarlet fever and typhoid fever were also prevalent. Diseases we don't think about today were deadly because this was before vaccines or antibiotics had been invented. There was, however, a plethora of patent medicines like Duffy's Pure Malt Whiskey, Fetzold's German Bitters, Guinn's Pioneer Blood Renewer and Awer's Ague Cure.

"The ladies from church sent over this soup, Mama. Do you think you could eat a little? It's your favorite, chicken and rice." Emily was lying on the mattress on the floor with a couple of ragged quilts on top of her. The only furniture in the room was the small table and a few chairs. Everything else had been sold. The clapboard walls were unpainted, had never been painted. The wood floor had no finish or covering of any kind. The ragged curtains at the window ballooned out as the wind came through the broken glass. As soon as she felt

The home of Dr. Sylvanus Ingram on Porter Street in Manchester, a few blocks from Emily's home. He treated Emily and her family from 1885 to 1886. It is now vacant and boarded up. *Benjamin Weiseger III.*

better, she would tape a piece of newspaper over the broken pane. But bare and stark as it was, the room was scrubbed clean. The fire in the stove was burning low, and there was a damp chill in the air, so Henry put a few more pieces of coal in. He wanted to keep his mama warm but knew they were short on coal. He walked across the room and knelt beside his mother; he propped her up on the coverless pillows and tucked the ragged quilts around her. Emily had been sick for almost a year. She had kept working as long as she could still stand—taking in laundry, cooking at the Possum lodge—but finally she gave out and had been in bed for weeks. The children had been sick off and on as well but had recovered more quickly. Although Maria was married and living with her family, she had come every day. Dr. Ingram had come to treat them, even though he knew they couldn't pay. But there was little he could do, since antibiotics had not been discovered yet. "I've just got to make up my mind to get up out of this bed and get back to work," Emily wheezed as she tried to get up and went into a fit of coughing that alarmed Henry. "That's OK, Mama, James and I are better now, and Bettie has started working again. You need to rest just a little while longer and let us take care of you." Emily managed a few sips of the soup. "Henry, tomorrow I want you to go see Mr. Cogbill and ask him to come see me. I need to ask him how we can get some money. I'm afraid we will need to sell the farm and even the house." "OK, Mama, I'll go right after work." Emily lay back down, wondering where they would go if they lost the house. Henry hurried back to work.

It was during this illness, and likely because of this illness, that Emily sold her properties. On June 29, 1886, she sold a building on her lot on Eighth Street to James McCullough for $475. The following day, she took out a loan on the property for $560, to be repaid over the next five years. This loan started Emily down the road that eventually led to her loss of the cottage. Here is an excerpt from that document:

> *In trust to secure to the holder of five certain negotiable notes of even date of this deed the payment of the sum of five hundred and sixty dollars ($560), said notes are at 1, 2, 3, 4 and 5 years, and for the sum of $106.00, $112.00, $118.00, $124.00 and the last note is for $100.00, are made by Emily Winfree by her endorsed and made negotiable and payable at the 1ˢᵗ National Bank of Richmond. In the event that default shall be made in the payment of either of the above mentioned notes as it becomes due and payable then the trustee when required to do so by the holder of said notes or either of them his executors, administrators, or assigns shall sell the property hereby conveyed. And it is covented and agreed between the parties aforesaid, that in case of a sale the same shall be made after first advertising the time, place and terms thereof, for ten days, in some newspaper published in the City of Richmond and upon the following terms to wit: for cash as to so much of the proceeds as may be necessary to defray the expenses of executing this trust, the fees for drawing and recording this deed, if then unpaid, and to discharge the amount of money then payable upon the said notes, and if at the time of such sale any of the said notes shall not have become due and payable, and the purchase money be sufficient, such part or parts of the said purchase money as will be sufficient to pay off and discharge such remaining notes shall be made payable at such time or times as the said remaining notes will become due, the payment of which part or parts shall be properly secured and in case the net proceeds of sale shall be applied towards the payment of the said notes in the order of their maturity, intending hereby to create a priority in favor of each said note over any other notes which may become due and payable subsequent thereto and if there be any residue of said purchase money, the same shall be made payable at such time, and secured in such manner, as the said parties of the first part her executors, administrators, or assigns, shall proscribe and direct, or in case of her failure to give such directive, at such time and in such manner as the said trustee shall think fit. The said party of the first part covenants to pay all taxes, assessments, dues and charges upon the said property hereby conveyed, so long as she or her heirs or assigns shall hold the same, and hereby waive*

the benefit of her Homestead Exemption as to the debt secured by this deed, and covenants to keep the improvements insured for at least $500.00, and in her default the trustee may insure at costs of grantor herein. If no default shall be made in the payment of the above mentioned notes then, upon the request of the party of the first part, a good and sufficient deed of release shall be executed to her at her own proper costs and charges.

At first glance, it seemed that both transactions (the sale and the loan) were for the same piece of property. Closer examination of the two contracts revealed that the original property had actually been divided into two pieces along Eighth Street. The piece she sold was only ten feet wide. She had been living in one structure and renting out the other. This explains how, when she petitioned the court to sell some timber off her farm, her trustee wrote that she was receiving rent from her property while she was living in it. Urban legend had it that she lived in one room of the two-room cottage and rented out the other room, but that is now debunked. In these two transactions, she sold one and took out a mortgage on the other, giving her a cash infusion of $1,035. We do not know how the money was spent.

Emily's legal affairs in dealing with her properties became very complicated and expensive. She could do nothing without her trustee, and by 1886, she was on her fifth one. She was charged lawyers' costs, commissioners' costs, court costs, taxes, filing fees and more every time she went to court. But it seemed she could do nothing without going to court—a catch-22. These transactions took a considerable chunk of her monies. Each time a trustee died, a new one had been appointed by the court. The last trustee was P.V. Cogbill. As trustee, Cogbill was required to petition the court each and every time a transaction was desired. He had to make regular financial reports to the court; he even needed permission to move funds from one bank to another if he wanted to get a better interest rate for her.

After the sale of the cottage in Manchester, Emily had to sell the 109.5 acres as well. Trustee Cogbill had to ask permission from the court to do so, and depositions were taken from experts who swore that the property was entirely unproductive; could not be rented out; had no habitable buildings; and that all parties would be best served if the land was sold and the money reinvested. Permission was granted to put the property up for auction, but there were no buyers.

Because the land did not sell, the court allowed a sale to a private individual, L.K. Woodbury, on September 8, 1887, for $1,100, to be paid in four yearly installments (Appendix IV). The court ordered a trust fund to be

By SAMPSON & ADAMSON,

Real Estate Auctioneers & Insurance Agents, 813 Hull St., Manchester, Va.

COMMISSIONERS' SALE

OF A VALUABLE

FARM

In Manchester Township, Chesterfield Co., Va.

In pursuance of a decree of the Circuit court of Chesterfield county, entered at its November term, 1886, in the chancery suit styled Emily Winfree and others *vs.* John Walker & others, the undersigned, Special Commissioners, will offer for sale, by Public Auction, in front of *CHESTERFIELD COURTHOUSE*, on

Monday, January 10th, 1887,

(that being Court-day), at **12** o'clock M., that valuable **FARM** known as Winfree's, with small FRAME HOUSE thereon, and containing 109½ acres of land, about 5 miles from Manchester, near Branch's church, and adjoining the Brookburry tract of land, now owned by Mr. Woodferny, the lands of Mr. — Robb and others. The Farm has upon it a splendid site for a *Grist Mill*, and its being so near the city should command the attention of parties desiring a really nice little Farm.

TERMS.—One-third cash, and balance payable in 1 2 and 3 years from day of sale, and title retained until the whole of the purchase money is paid and conveyance ordered by the cou.

SAMPSON & ADAMSON, Auctioneers.

THOS. M. MILLER,
P. V. COGBILL,
Special Commissioners.

A broadside for an auction of Emily's farm in 1887. Note the mention of the small house that she built there in 1867. *Library of Virginia.*

set up for Emily at the State Bank of Virginia, and a $300 down payment was deposited there. Mr. Woodbury made the required payments for his purchase of the farm. His payments were deposited into Emily's trust.

By July 1889, Emily had missed three payments on her deed of trust, for a total of $357.12. Since Woodbury had been making the payments on the

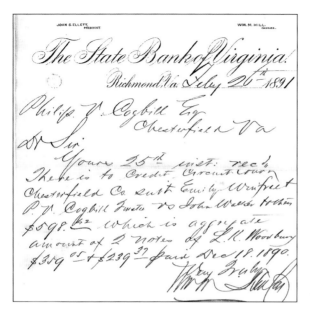

A receipt for some of the payments for the farm by Woodbury into Emily's trust at the State Bank of Virginia. *Library of Virginia.*

farm, there was now $399.72 in the trust fund. Cogbill received permission from the court to take the money out of the trust fund to pay the overdue notes, leaving $42.60.

In December 1889, poor Dr. Ingram still had not been paid, so he petitioned the court, with Emily's verbal consent, to take the $36 that Emily still owed him from her trust. We don't know if his request was granted. On September 20, 1890, Woodbury had paid off all his notes on the land, and Emily signed over the deed. Now she had no more money coming in from that quarter. In 1891, Emily was again behind in her payments, so Cogbill once more obtained permission to use money from her trust to pay them off. Throughout all of this, there is every indication that Cogbill was trying to do his best for Emily, but court costs and trustee fees depleted her meager funds significantly. As an example of her costs, in November 1887, Cogbill submitted a report of his expenses including taxes, filing fees, commissioner fees and attorney fees that totaled $211.68, a significant sum. Remember that Emily only received $1,100 for the farm and $475 for the cottage. She also owed the money on the deed of trust.

Somehow, in 1893, Emily had enough money to buy a house in the new section of Marx's Addition on Stockton Street, a few blocks from the cottage. Perhaps the children were now contributing to her funds. The new house was much larger than the cottage. Cogbill asked the court's permission to use some of the money from the sale of the land for the down payment. The

A note from David Branch to Emily, April 27, 1893: "Dear Emily, Yours dated the 11th inst. & mailed in Manchester the 24th inst. reached me the 25th with enclosures. I have very cheerfully signed the papers & return it to you in this. Glad I could be of that much service to you. Hope you will get it promptly & in good time. Respectfully, D.P. Branch." *Library of Virginia.*

court agreed, but with the stipulation that all of David's heirs relinquish any claim they might have to the money. It is not clear why that was necessary, because the deed for the property that David gave to Emily in 1866 clearly stated that she could do anything she wanted with both of her properties, including selling them and reinvesting the money. Fortunately, the heirs agreed to give up any claims they had, and the court determined that the house on Stockton was a good investment for Emily. In the large file we found at the Library of Virginia regarding Emily's land dealings, we found the note that David's nephew David Branch had written to her: "Dear Emily, Yours dated the 11th inst. & mailed in Manchester the 24th inst. reached me the 25th with enclosures. I have very cheerfully signed the paper & return it to you in this. Glad I could be of that much service to you. Hope you will get it promptly & in good time. Respectfully, D.P. Branch."

This is a very important note. David Branch and Emily were contemporaries. They grew up together in the Branch household and were similar in age. It appears that they remained friendly over the years,

The house at 1515 Stockton Street, Manchester, as it looks today. Emily purchased it in 1893 and lived there until her death in 1919. *Authors' photograph.*

and David responded to Emily's request immediately and cheerfully. This suggests familiarity and even affection. We have even considered that David Branch may have been Maria's father, all those years ago. He was at least Maria's cousin.

Imagine what it must have been like to have so little control over your own life. Emily was not trusted to make her own decision to sell her land and buy a house. She had to ask the court's permission to do so. The house she bought is still standing on the corner of Sixteenth and Stockton Streets in Manchester (1515 Stockton). She lived there until her death.

In 1898, Emily's daughter Lucy bought the property right next to Emily's. She lived there until she married Charles Hicks in 1901. After their divorce, she moved in with Emily.

Our next record of Emily's affairs is the 1900 census, because the 1890 census was destroyed by fire. We find Emily, James, Henry, Clifford and a new daughter, Lucy, living together. Although we have mentioned Lucy in the preceding paragraph, this is the first time she showed up in a census. She was born around 1877/78, and we first see her when she is about twenty because of the missing 1890 census. The identity of her father is not known. It surely could not have been David, because he had been dead for ten years prior to her birth. However, he is listed as her father on her death certificate many years later. Emily was shown for the first time as head of household, rather than being employed, so perhaps she was no longer working and the children were caring for her. Walter and his wife lived a block away. Maria and her husband, John Walker, also lived close.

On July 17, 1905, even though Emily had paid off the loan on the house using funds from her trust, back taxes had accrued until the amount owed was greater than the value of the house, so the court had her and all her children sign it over to F.P. Pettigrew for the sums of one dollar to Emily and one dollar to each of the children (Appendix V). We don't know if he had been renting the house from her, but he was definitely living in it in 1907.

Except for Bettie, all the children stayed close. She had married the white gentleman Mr. Albert Merrifield in 1889 and moved to Providence, Rhode Island. She lived there the rest of her life, and Rhode Island census records list her, her husband and her daughter, Emily, all as white.

December 1918—one month before Emily's death
Emily was curled up on her favorite chair in front of the fireplace. It was old and tattered but very cushy, and she loved snuggling down in the cushions. It seemed she was cold all the time now, so James had come over and built a crackling fire for her. Her old dog, Boomer, lay at her feet. It seemed that the both of them were old and stiff now—and always cold. She had brought him home as a bedraggled pup so many years ago, even though she could barely afford to feed herself and the family. They were constant companions now. The boys had moved her bed from upstairs to the dining room so she wouldn't have to climb the stairs. She felt so weary, but she just couldn't stay in bed all day. Lucy had her all snuggled up in the warmest quilts in the house, and she was sitting there in silence while Lucy prepared dinner.

Emily knew this had been her last Christmas, and she thanked God for every moment. The whole family had come. Even Bettie and Albert and little Emily had driven down from Rhode Island. It had taken them three days, but they finally pulled in on Christmas Eve. They stayed with Clifford and Martha over on Porter Street. Emily had sat and watched the family from her chair, too ill to participate. She had felt like a spirit, detached from the scene, just watching the merry family as they prepared dinner. There were so many of them that they had to fork and spoon and ladle the food right out of the pots in the kitchen, and they were spread out, chatting and eating all over the house and into the backyard. They had splurged and bought some of those new-fangled paper plates because they didn't have enough dishes for everybody. The entire home was filled with happy, loving chatter. How grateful she was.

But now it was quiet. Bettie and her family had left yesterday, and Emily knew she would never see her daughter or namesake granddaughter again. She spent her time now reflecting on her life. How far she had come from being Jordan Branch's slave in Petersburg. That seemed like a million years ago. Now, here she sat in a comfortable, two-story house they owned outright. Oh, they weren't well off by any means, but they weren't in constant fear of starving or losing their home anymore. And all seven children except one lived right here in Richmond. Bettie had been so determined to get out of here, and Emily guessed she was happy up there, living as a white woman. She knew she had advantages that the others didn't have. She wrote letters to Emily from time to time, and Lucy read them to her. After Maria's husband, John, died, she had moved in with her daughter. Maria had always been the strong one, the second mother to the family, and now she was taking care of grandchildren while the parents worked. And all but one of the grandchildren were here too. She thought about all the people she knew who had lost their whole families and never found them after the war. She was so much luckier than most. All of the children were making their ways honestly. Walter was still angry all the time, though. He said that no matter how hard he tried, he never felt like a real man. Some time ago, he tried a couple of times to register to vote. Clifford had taught him to read, and he studied some, but no matter what he had learned, it was always the wrong thing. Those white men always thought of some way to humiliate him and ask him something he couldn't answer. He finally stopped trying, too embarrassed to go back. Henry and James never did try. Clifford, even though he was a teacher, never got to register.

James and Henry never married, but they both had steady work most of the time. Every time they changed jobs she had panicked, afraid they would get arrested for vagrancy and end up in prison or on the chain gang. Clifford and Lucy, the two youngest, both had the chance to finish school, and they were both principals in the Manchester colored schools. Clifford was a leader in the church and a successful businessman. He and others had started an insurance company for the colored folks. This was very successful because up until then, all those insurance companies owned by white people were a constant nuisance *to us, going around knocking on our doors all the time. And Lucy, she had even gone to Hampton Institute—she was the most educated of all the children.*

Emily would sometimes reflect on the time she spent with David, all those years ago. She found that she couldn't talk about those feelings, so she just pondered them in silence. She and David had had most of these children "together." But it wasn't like they were married and said, "Let's raise a big family together." She hadn't had a choice, so by definition their relationship was abusive. She had never had the chance to choose a husband. But they and their children were a family, whether it was said out loud or not. He was a part of them. All of their lives, she could see him in them; the way James walked, the strength of Maria, Henry's hazel eyes. And she loved every one of those children, so how was it possible to hate their father? Nobody had forced David to give her the little house and the land. That was his idea, and she was very grateful for it. During the hardest times, those properties were the only thing that stood between her and homelessness or starvation. So what were her true feelings about David now, fifty-one years after his death? She guessed it was a kind of mixture of loathing and love, constantly sparring, but neither winning a decided victory. What difference did it make now, anyway? She hadn't made it this far by worrying about things she couldn't change. And she had made it! She knew now that the family was a success, and she knew that her children would raise successful children, and they would in turn raise successful children, and on and on it would go, getting better and better with each generation. Someday things would change, not for her, and not for her children, but for their children. And she would be looking down, watching over them and sending messages to urge them on, rejoicing in their successes. Emily was tired. She had done her best, and her story was ended. But she felt nothing but pride and hopefulness for the future of this family. She was content. She was ready to be called home.

Emily Winfree was finally called home on January 10, 1919, of "natural causes incident to old age." On the certificate of death, her marital status is "widow"; her occupation is "domestic"; her parents are John W. Scott and Emily Jones, both born in Virginia; the informant is her son Clifford; and the undertaker is C.S. Cunningham. Her son James bought a family plot in Mount Olivet Cemetery (now part of Maury Cemetery), and she is buried there along with sons Henry, Clifford and James; daughters Mariah and Lucy; and Clifford's wife, Martha.

We can imagine the scene. Bettie probably arrived from Rhode Island. They would not have had the funeral service in the same church they had visited for David's service. It would have been in a smaller, inelegant building. After the service, the family would have followed Emily up to the African American cemetery, Mount Olivet. Their plot was on the top of a lovely hill. Many tears would have been shed and many stories told of her

Above: Emily's grave marker in Maury Cemetery, Manchester. *Authors' photograph.*

Opposite: A copy of Emily Winfree's death certificate, 1919. *Commonwealth of Virginia.*

strength in the worst situations. They had all pitched in to buy an obelisk inscribed with the words "Beloved Mother." Emily deserved to rest. She had struggled for so many years to keep this family intact. So many families had been separated or destroyed by everything that had happened during her lifetime. Her children probably knew men or boys who had been sent to prison, perhaps died there. Yet here they were—all alive, all employed, all with homes. They knew what they owed her, and they would pay that forward to the coming generations of the Winfree clan. Afterward, they went down to the home at 1515 Stockton Street and celebrated her victory.

The small cottage in which this story played out, the 476 square feet in which Emily raised her children, still sits on rails in Shockoe Bottom, next to Lumpkin's Jail site. It is time that it is restored as a historical landmark for African American history in Richmond, Virginia.

Chapter 11

THE LEGACY

The story of Emily Winfree does not end with her death. After we had learned all we could about her life, we set out to find her descendants. We were very lucky; we found thirty-three who are living today. Their stories are Emily's true legacy.

Emily's Children

Maria Winfree Walker (1856–1936)

Of all of Emily's children, we know the most about Maria, better known as Grandma "Moosh" by her great-granddaughter Emily Grace Jones Jefferson. She was born into slavery but lived her adult life as a free person. She had been compelled to become industrious and strong-willed by the circumstances of her childhood. At eleven, she was keeping house and minding her younger siblings while her mother worked. Later, she was a laundress. She married John H. Walker in 1878. On her marriage license, David Winfree was named as her father. We know that Maria had a son prior to her marriage to John, but we do not know the father. The baby boy was named Burfoot, the same name as one of David Winfree's nephews, in whose house she did laundry. Maria and John Walker had six children: John

Maria Winfree Walker, Emily's eldest child. *Robert Goins Jr.*

(1879), Pattie (1881), Mary Elizabeth (1883), James (1884), Benjamin (1889) and Emily (1891). Sometime after her husband's death, Maria lived with her daughter Mary Elizabeth Jones and her family and became "Grandma Moosh." She was a defining force in the lives of her grandchildren, all of whom were notably successful. Maria died of apoplexy (stroke) on December 8, 1936. On her death certificate, her father was listed as "unknown."

Elizabeth Winfree Merrifield (1859–1938)

Bettie was born enslaved to David Winfree. She was the only one of Emily's children who left Richmond. She married Albert Merrifield, a white man from New England, and lived as a white woman in Providence, Rhode Island. She had one daughter, Emily, who also lived as a white woman.

Walter David Winfree (1862–1946)

Walter married Ella Irving and had one daughter, Fannie. He worked at various jobs in his life, including upholsterer and janitor. We found one record in the newspaper of his arrest for fighting with the in-laws of his brother Clifford. Luckily, he was only fined and not imprisoned. Judges were lenient on Black-on-Black crimes. Walter died of influenza and chronic interstitial nephritis. On his death certificate, his father was listed as David Winfree.

James Wiley Winfree (1865–1937)

James was named after David's father. He worked as a cook and a waiter. He never married, but he bought the family plot and Emily's gravestone in Mount Olivet Cemetery. James died of apoplexy (stroke). On his death certificate, his father was listed as David Winfree.

Henry Winfree (1866–1949)

Henry worked most of his life as a laborer and a waiter. He never married. Henry died of pneumonia and generalized arteriosclerosis. On his death certificate, his father was listed as David Winfree.

Clifford Louis Winfree (1869–1936)

Clifford became a community leader. In 1896, he and others started an insurance company for the African American community. The *Richmond Planet* reported this with the commentary, "God grant that they may meet with success for our people are tired of white insurance agents knocking at their doors." Clifford was director of the Sunday school at his church and became a teacher and then principal in the Manchester colored schools. He married Martha Waddell and had four children: Clifford, Robert, James Collins and Lacontess. We have been unable to trace their descendants. Clifford died on July 10, 1936, of a cerebral hemorrhage. On his death certificate, his father was listed as David Winfree.

Lucy Winfree Hicks Taylor (1877/78–1941)

Lucy went to Hampton Institute and became a teacher in the Manchester colored schools. She married Charles Hicks in 1901 and had two sons, Walter and Alvin. Later, Lucy divorced Hicks and married Herbert Taylor. Lucy died of cerebral apoplexy (stroke). On her death certificate, her father was listed as David Winfry, but he had been dead for ten years at the time of her birth.

EMILY'S GRANDCHILDREN

The grandchildren are listed in full in the previous entries about their parents. We have only two pictures.

Mary Elizabeth Walker Jones (1883–?) was a teacher. She married Walter D. Jones, and they had six children: Stephen, Cornelia, Mary Lydia, Walter Douglas, John Robert and Emily Grace. They were a respected family in Jackson Ward.

Alvin Lionel Hicks (1905–1990)

Top: Mary Elizabeth Walker Jones, Maria Walker's daughter and Emily's granddaughter. *Robert Goins Jr. Bottom*: Alvin Lionel Hicks, Lucy Winfree Hicks Taylor's son and Emily's grandson. *Charles Hicks Sr.*

EMILY'S GREAT-GRANDCHILDREN

Of Emily's great-grandchildren, we know the most about the children of Maria's daughter Mary Elizabeth Walker Jones. These were the six curious children with whom we opened the story. We now find them many years later, all grown up. The second generation out of slavery, they took full advantage of the opportunities provided them. All graduated from Armstrong High School in Richmond, and all attended Virginia Union University. Three of them were part of the mass movement of African Americans out of the South, the Great Migration.

Stephen Douglas Jones (1915–2008)

Of all six Jones children, Stephen looked the most like Emily. He attended Virginia Union University. Drafted into the army during World War II, he was promoted to second lieutenant. The insignias on his lapels state that he was in the cavalry, which was mostly mechanized during World War II. All of the armed forces were still segregated then, and Black officers were uncommon. He must have been outstanding at his work to become an officer. After the war, Stephen worked as a postal employee, and as a retired gentleman, he taught handicapped children how to swim. He was married to Velta Carter. They had no children.

Stephen Douglas Jones, Mary Jones's son and Emily's great-grandson. *Robert Goins Jr.*

Mary Lydia Walker Jones Pollard (Aunt Mae, 1920–2016)

Mary was named the most outstanding high school female athlete in Richmond. After graduating from Virginia Union University, she married Charles Nathaniel Pollard and had two children, Charles Jr. and Charlean. Widowed by World War II at a young age, she sometimes stayed with her mother's family at 814 West Marshall Street. Mary was a substitute teacher in Richmond and a fashion model for Thalhimers and Miller & Rhoads department stores.

Mary Lydia Jones Pollard, Mary Jones's daughter and Emily's great-granddaughter. *Robert Goins Jr.*

Cornelia Walker Jones Goins (1918–1986)

Cornelia Walker Jones Goins, Mary Jones's daughter and Emily's great-granddaughter. *Robert Goins Jr.*

Cornelia graduated from Virginia Union University and later earned an MA degree from Virginia State University. She married Robert Goins Sr., another teacher. They both taught in a Rosenwald school in the Lynchburg area. Between 1915 and 1929, Julius Rosenwald, president of Sears, Roebuck and Co., built over five thousand schools across the South that provided access to education for 660,000 African American children. He was inspired to do this after meeting Booker T. Washington. Cornelia was a teacher, and her husband was the principal of their school. She taught for thirty-six years in the Lynchburg area. She and Robert had two children, Robert Jr. and Cornelia.

John Robert Douglas Jones (Uncle Jack, 1924–1992)

John was a conductor, pianist and music educator. After serving in the Thirty-Seventh Special Service in the army during World War II, John moved to New York City, where he attended New York University and bartended at his family business, the Red Rooster, a New York institution. John would continue his education and earn a master's degree at Manhattan School of Music and eventually begin his career as a music educator for the New York City Department of Education. While working for the NYC DOE, John conducted choirs at Alice Tully Hall and Carnegie Hall, as well as led parades down Seventh Avenue in Harlem in honor of Marcus Garvey. He dovetailed his career with the NYC DOE by earning his EDD at NYU, elevating the works of one of his musical heroes, Undine Smith Moore. John met his last wife, Maggie

John Robert Douglas Jones, Mary Jones's son and Emily's great-grandson. *Robert Goins Jr.*

Funderburk Toles, when they were both teaching in the Bronx. When he married Maggie, they moved with her daughter Michelle to New Jersey, where they welcomed their younger daughter Emily Joy.

Walter Douglas Jones Jr. (Uncle Pete, 1922–2008)

Walter Douglas Jones Jr., Mary Jones's son and Emily's great-grandson. *Robert Goins Jr.*

Walter was an acclaimed secondary school teacher and university professor who lived in Michigan and later Ohio. After graduating from Virginia Union University, he received his master's degree from New York University and did postgraduate studies at Wayne State University in Detroit. He received many awards for his contributions to social and civil groups. He was featured in *Personalities of the South* in 1971, published by the American Biographical Institute. He was married to Thelma Jeffries and had one son, Michael.

Emily Grace Jones Jefferson (1926–present)

Emily Grace Jones Jefferson, Mary Jones's daughter and Emily's great-granddaughter. *Robert Goins Jr.*

Emily graduated from Virginia Union University, where she met and later married Donald Jefferson, who had a PhD in engineering. They had two children, Eleanor and Donald. They made their home in Maryland, and she became a librarian at the Library of Congress in Washington, D.C. She is the only living family member who knew Maria Winfree Walker, and she has wonderful memories of her "Grandma Moosh." When we first discovered these relatives of Emily, the president of the Virginia Museum of History and Culture, Jamie Bosket, sent a letter to each one, and we followed up with a phone call two weeks later. On my first several calls, nobody knew who Emily Winfree was. On my last call, an elderly lady answered the phone. When I asked her if she had received the letter from Jamie, she acknowledged that she had. When I asked if she had ever heard of Emily Winfree, she replied, "I know who Emily Winfree is. I was named after her." After that marvelous moment, we had several long conversations, during which she related the tales about "Moosh" that you have read. When we had a reunion for the family at the Virginia Museum of History and Culture, I was giving a PowerPoint presentation to the family members about Emily. Near the end, the picture of Maria flashed up, and Emily Grace gasped. She had not known we had it. Both of us choked up, and I had to wait a minute before I was able to continue. The part Emily Grace played in bringing this story to life cannot be overstated.

Maria Grace Cogbill Wilson (1908–1984)

Maria Grace was Maria's granddaughter through her daughter Pattie. She was a teacher. She married George Wilson and had one child, Sylvia Wilson Ritchie, who provided this picture and told us her mom often helped out with all of the Jones children.

Maria Grace Cogbill, Pattie Walker Cogbill's daughter and Emily's great-granddaughter. *Sylvia Ritchie.*

THE FAMILY TODAY

The current generation of Emily's descendants hails from Michigan; New Jersey; Maryland; Washington, D.C.; Lynchburg, Virginia; and Midlothian, Virginia. They have taken full advantage of their inheritance: intelligence, fortitude and the will to succeed. Among them are four who have obtained PhDs in science, education and engineering; a high school counselor; one who started his own radio station; a track star who received a full scholarship to Michigan State University and later became a coach; and several highly successful business owners. Thirty-three of them were invited to the Virginia Museum of History and Culture in July 2018 for a family reunion, where they were given a presentation of what we have learned about their ancestor. They represented two branches of Emily's family: descendants of Emily's oldest daughter, Maria, and her youngest daughter, Lucy. The two branches of the family had never met until that day. What a pleasure it was to watch them as they became acquainted. After a catered

Descendants of Emily Winfree examining documents provided during a reunion held at the Virginia Museum of History and Culture. *Authors' photograph.*

Descendants of Emily Winfree in front of her cottage in Shockoe Bottom. *Authors' photograph.*

luncheon, they were bused about town and shown the home where Emily last lived in Manchester, her grave in the family plot in Maury Cemetery and the little dilapidated cottage where this story unfolded. It is the single remaining structure of its kind in Richmond. We stay in touch with them and hope to work together to get the cottage recognized for its historical importance.

EPILOGUE

*E*mily Winfree was the embodiment of the strength of character it took to face the struggles and injustices of her time and place. She never succumbed, always praying for the time when the yoke would be lifted. It did not happen for her. She never got an education, never voted, never worked at a good-paying job, never rode in the front of a bus, if she indeed ever rode a bus. She lived in constant fear that her sons would be arrested, her daughters raped. In spite of all these disadvantages, she succeeded. The generations that came after her not only look like her, but they also exhibit her traits: intelligence, love of family, the drive to succeed, love of learning. They are her legacy.

Emily's story goes beyond Emily. It speaks for the millions of African American women and men whose stories will never be told, whose names have been lost but who must not be forgotten. The number of original documents we found in our search for Emily's story is very unusual. It is very difficult to find verifiable facts about enslaved people. Last names were rarely recorded, and first names could be incorrect or commonly were names assigned by masters. Witness the fact that, although we found so much, we never could find out exactly when, where or to whom Emily was born.

The discrimination and suppression that Emily Winfree and millions of others endured have not been wholly resolved in Richmond, Virginia. The Jones home at 814 West Marshall Street was destroyed in the 1950s when I-95 was run through Jackson Ward, effectively destroying that prosperous African American neighborhood. Emily Grace went to the house before the bulldozers arrived and saved some of the family papers, but many were lost. Many of the people who lost their single-family homes were herded into public housing communities that are, today, the center of most of the poverty and crime in the city, with little or no access to grocery stores, jobs, public transportation and such necessities. Even after *Brown v. Board of Education* and school integration, the city's public schools are primarily African American and chronically underfunded. Newspaper stories tell of pieces of ceiling falling on children's heads. It is telling that none of Maria Winfree Walker's descendants stayed in Richmond.

Now that the story of Emily Winfree's family and the cottage in which they lived is told, Richmonders have the golden opportunity to get the cottage off the rails on which it sits, find a home for it and restore it as a testament to the fortitude of Emily and a monument to all those who have been forgotten. It could become an educational venue for African American history in Richmond.

DEED TO HOUSE IN MANCHESTER

This deed made this 16th day of March 1866 between Samual E. Vadin, party of the first part, and A.A. Allen trustee of the second part, and Emily Winfree and her children (colored persons) parties of the third part: witnesseth that the party of the first part in consideration of the sum of eight hundred dollars grants with general warranty unto the party of the second part that certain parcel of land lying in the town of Manchester part of a certain lot distinguished in the plans of said town by the number two hundred and fifteen (215) fronting seventy five (75) feet on the eastern line of Allen Street, commencing at the line of the lots recently conveyed by the party of the first part to Francis J. Sampson, which line is fifty (50) feet from the corner of Porter and Allen streets and running back between parallel lines one hundred and thirty two (132) feet. In trust however for the benefit of said Emily Winfree and her children during her life time. With remainder at her death to her children and their descendants surviving her, said descendants taking per stirpes and upon further trust that the said Emily Winfree may at her discretion during her lifetime sell the property and invest the proceeds in other real property and in such sale and commission the trustee shall unite with the said Emily Winfree in conveying the title to the property sold; shall advise with her as to the investment of the proceeds causing the title of the property purchased to be taken in his name as trustee subject to the limitations and trusts of this deed. And upon further trust that in the event

Copy of original deed signed March 14, 1866, for the cottage David Winfree gave to Emily Winfree. *Chesterfield County Courthouse.*

that the said Emily Winfree shall die without children or issue surviving her the property shall pass to such persons as she shall by will direct and appoint. And in default of making such will the same shall pass to said David C. Winfree.

Appendix II

DEED TO ACREAGE

This deed made this 29th day of May AD 1866 between David C. Winfree party of the first part, A.A. Allen party of the second part, and Emily Winfree a colored woman and her children parties of the third part. Witnesseth that the party of the first part grants unto the said party of the second part that certain parcel of land lying in the County of Chesterfield, part of the same land conveyed to the said D.C. Winfree by Povall Turner and wife and described in a certain survey and plan and tract of land made by D. LaPrade, surveyor of Powhatan County dated 10 Nov 1865 for said (Dr.) D.C. Winfree as follows. Commencing at corner rock in [now Smith and M.L. Blankenship] S. 22 feet' & 11 chains 5 links to the corner Black Oak thence N. 88' & 7 chains to corner stake, thence S. 21' & 22 chains 25 links to stake, thence S. 76.5' & 65 chains to hickory; thence 6.5' W a short distance to the creek; thence up the creek as it meanders to the first abrupt bend in the course of the creek (the creek at this point ascending the stream diverging northward and almost forming a right angle); thence from said creek for a short distance N. 56.5' to a black oak; thence N. 13.5 E & across the creek to a brick on the opposite side of the creek; thence due north to James H. Walker's line; thence S 79.5' & 53 chains, 37 links along said Walker's line to a rock; thence S. 72.5' & 36 chains 10 links to the point of beginning, containing according to said survey made by D. LaPrade one hundred & nine & one half acres. But this grant is made upon trust for the sole and exclusive benefit and use of the said Emily Winfree and her children during her lifetime with remainder at her death

Copy of original deed signed May 29, 1866, for the 109.5-acre farm David Winfree gave to Emily Winfree. *Chesterfield County Courthouse.*

to her children then surviving her and the descendants of any who may have died leaving issue, such descendants taking per stirpes, but should the said Emily Winfree die without leaving issue or children surviving her then said land shall revert to the said David C. Winfree. But the said Emily Winfree shall be entitled to occupy and use the land or to rent or lease the same and to collect and receive the rents into her own proper hands and apply the same under the provisions of this deed; and she is also authorized and empowered to sell the said land and invest the proceeds of sale in other real property and the title to the property so purchased shall be taken to be held in trust subject to the limitations, trusts and provisions of this deed; and in making any such sale the trustee shall, at the request of the said Emily Winfree unite with her by a sufficient deed in making title to the purchaser; and such sale and conversion may be repeatedly made as often as the said Emily Winfree may deem advisable. Witness the following signatures and seals   D.C. Winfree.

Appendix III

PETITION TO SELL TIMBER
FROM ACREAGE AND BUILD HOUSE

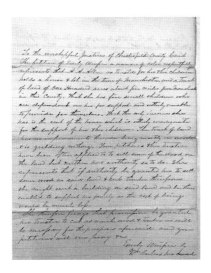

Copy of petition asking permission for Emily to cut timber off her acreage to build a house after David's death in 1867. *Library of Virginia.*

To the worshipful justices of Chesterfield County Court. The petition of Emily Winfree a woman of color respectfully represents that A.A. Allen as trustee for her & her children holds a house & lot in the town of Manchester, and a tract of land of one hundred acres about four miles from Manchester in this County. That she has five small children who are dependent on her for support and utterly unable to provide for themselves. That the only income she has is the rent of the house which is utterly inadequate for the support of her & her children. The tract of land has no improvements thereon being mostly in woods & is yielding nothing. Your petitioner & this trustee have been often [illegible] to sell some of the wood on the land, but neither has authority to do so. She represents that if authority be granted her to sell some wood on said land & cut timber therefrom she might erect a building on said land and be thus enabled to support her family as the cost of living would be much less.

She therefore prays that permission be granted her trustee to cut as much wood & timber as will be necessary for the purposes aforesaid and your petitioner will ever pray to.

Emily Winfree by William Ambers

I concur in the petition asked for by Emily Winfree and think no other way can keep her & her children from suffering.

A. Allen by William Ambers her counsel.

DEED FOR SALE OF ACREAGE TO WOODBURY

This deed made this 20th day of September 1890 between Philip V. Cogbill, substituted trustee and special commissioner of the Circuit Court of Chesterfield County as hereinafter explained party of the first part Emily Winfree (a colored woman) party of the second part L.K. Woodbury party of the third part and Clara M. Woodbury (who is the wife of the said L.K. Woodbury) party of the fourth part. Witnesseth: That whereas David C. Winfree by his deed dated the 29th day of May 1866 and recorded in deed book No. 48 at page 123 in Chesterfield County Courthouse conveyed unto A.A. Allen trustee for Emily Winfree (a colored woman) and her children the tract of land hereinafter mentioned and described and conveyed upon certain trusts and provisions set forth in the said deed as follows: to wit:

And whereas the said Emily Winfree deeming it advisable and to the advantage of all parties concerned to make sale of the said land and invest the proceeds in other property as provided in said deed, but there being no trustee to execute a proper conveyance, the said A.A. Allen trustee having been substituted as such by J.M. Moody who died and who was substituted by H.W. Branford who likewise died and the said Emily Winfree preferring that such a sale should be made and the proceeds invested under and by direction of the Court of Chancery wherein the rights of all parties would be more fully protected instituted a chancery suit for the purpose in the Circuit Court of Chesterfield County wherein the same is now pending under the short style of "Emily Winfree vs. John Walker et al." And whereas the said Court by its decree of said cause entered on the 23rd day of November 1886 appointed the said P.V. Cogbill trustee in the place and stead of said H.W. Branford deceased. And by its decree entered in said cause on the 24th day of November 1886, directed the said P.V. Cogbill substituted trustee and J.M. Miller who was thereby appointed special commissioner for the purpose with authority to either or both of whom to act to make sale of the said land (hereinafter described) under the terms and in the manner by said decree described. And whereas the said special commissioner having failed (though they endeavored so to do) to make sale of the same at public auction the said P.V. Cogbill special commissioner, on the 8th day of September, 1887 made private sale of the said land (as authorized by the said last mentioned decree) to the said L.K. Woodbury at the price of eleven hundred dollars upon the following terms to wit. Three hundred dollars cash, three hundred dollars payable twelve months from said date with interest from date, three hundred dollars payable two years from said date with like interest, and two hundred dollars payable three years from said date with like interest. Said deferred payments evidenced by the negotiable notes of said L.K. Woodbury payable at the State Bank of Virginia, the said cash payments and the notes for deferred payments to be deposited in said bank to the credit of said Court in said cause and the title to be retained until the payments of the purchase money and a conveyance ordered by the Court, and having made report of said sale the said Court by its decree entered in said cause on

Left and opposite: Copy of deed Emily gave to Woodbury after he made all payments for the 109.5-acre farm. *Chesterfield County Courthouse.*

the 24th day of September 1887 duly confirmed the said sale. And whereas the decree entered in said cause on the 11th day of September 1890 it was ordered and directed that upon payment by the said L.K. Woodbury into the State Bank of Virginia as provided by said decree of November 24, 1886 of the balance of the purchase money of said land, the said P.V. Cogbill as substituted trustee as aforesaid and as special commissioner of the said Court thereby appointed for the purpose upon satisfactory evidence of such payments being exhibited to him do execute and deliver unto the said L.K. Woodbury or to such other person as said L.K. Woodbury may designate a good and sufficient deed conveying unto him or such other persons with special warranty of title the said tract of 109.5 acres of land, and said Emily Winfree shall join in such conveyance.

And whereas the said L.K. Woodbury has paid the balance of said purchase money into said bank and exhibited to said P.V. Cogbill, substituted trustee and special commissioner satisfactory evidence of such payment and has requested that the deed for said land be executed to the said Clara M. Woodbury his wife as evidenced by his becoming a party to and signing this deed.

And the said L.K. Woodbury hereby grants and conveys unto the said Clara M. Woodbury with general warranty all his right title and interest in the said tract of land. Witness the following signatures and seals.
State of Virginia

Opposite and following two pages: Copy of petition in which Emily and all her children relinquished all interest in her cottage, which went to A.N. Pettigrew. *Richmond City Court Records.*

PETITION BY EMILY AND ALL HER CHILDREN TO PAY OFF ALL DEED OF TRUST NOTES BUT GIVE UP THE COTTAGE DUE TO BACK TAXES

Emily Winfree, etc.

vs.

Walker et als.

   To the Honorable Walter A. Watson, Judge of the Circuit Court for the County of Chesterfield, Virginia:-

     The undersigned, your petitioners, beg leave to file this their petition, and show unto the Court the following facts, to-wit: That there has been pending in your Honorable Court, since the year 1886, a chancery suit under the short style of Emily Winfree etc. vs. John Walker et als, the said suit having been brought for the purpose of selling a tract of land in the County of Chesterfield; that your petitioner, Emily Winfree is the plaintiff in the said suit, and that your other petitioners are the defendants in said suit and are the children of said Emily Winfree, namely, Walter D. Winfree and his wife, Ella Winfree, James W. Winfree, Henry Winfree, Clifford L. Winfree and his wife, Martha E. Winfree, Mariah Walker and her husband John Walker, she being formerly Mariah Winfree, Lucy J. Hicks and Chas. Hicks, her husband, she being formerly Lucy J. Winfree, and Elizabeth Merrifield and ~~Alfred~~ Albert E. Merrifield, her husband, she being formerly Elizabeth Winfree; that is thus shown some of the said children have married since the institution of the suit aforesaid, and that all of them are now over the age of 21 years, and that the aforesaid persons are all of the children of the said Emily Winfree, none of said Emily Winfree's children ever having died since the institution of said suit, and also being all of the respective wives and husbands of said children; that

by deed dated March 14, 1866, and recorded in the Clerk's Office
of your honorable Court in D.B. 48, page 18, one Sam'l E. Vaden
conveyed to Emily Winfree's trustee, A.A.Allen, (and her children's
a lot of land on Eighth street, fronting 75 feet thereon, in the
City of Manchester, Va.; that by deed dated June 30, 1886, and
recorded in D.B. 7, page 2, in the Clerk's Office of the Corporation
Court of Manchester, said Emily Winfree conveyed said lot of land
in Manchester to R.B.Taylor, trustee, to secure the holder of the
hereinafter mentioned notes the sum of $560.; that only said Emily
Winfree signed said deed of trust, no trustee joining therein; that
a part of the purchase money, received from the sale of the tract of
land in said suit mentioned and described, was used by your honorable Court to take up the said notes secured as above stated, there
being altogether five of them; that the said notes are all dated
June 30, 1886, and are payable respectively 1, 2, 3, 4, and 5
years after date, at the 1st. Natioanl Bank of Richmond, Va., and
are for the respective sums of $106., $112. $118. $124., and the
fifth one for $100., the total sum being $560.00; that the said
notes are filed with the papers in the said cause, the first three,
namely, the notes for $106., for $112. and for $118. are filed and
returned with the report of P.V.Cogbill, substituted trustee, which
said report was filed in the said cause on the 11th. day of Sept.,
1890, and the last two, namely, the notes for $124. and $100., respectively, are filed and returned with the report of P.V.Cogbill,
substituted trustee, which said report was filed in the said cause
on the 23rd. day of Nov., 1891; that the said five notes were pur-

chased by the Court as an investment, but that the same are now
practically valuelesss, because the property upon which the said
deed of trust is a lien has over $500.00 State and City taxes due
upon it, which sum is about all that the property is worth; that
your petitioners realizing that the said notes and the said lot of
land in Manchester were of little value to them, have conveyed all
of their rights and interests in said lot to Mr. A. N. Pettigrew,
for a valuable consideration, as is evidenced by a deed signed by
your said petitioners, dated July 17, 1905, and recorded or to be
in the Clerk's office of Manchester; and that, therefore, none of
your said petitioners claim or assert any interest or estate in
the said property in Manchester, nor any interest in or claim upon
upon the said notes, secured as above described, and are willing
to and do hereby relinquish any right or interest that they may
have in said notes.

the said property in Manchester, nor any interest in or claim upon upon the said notes, secured as above described, and are willing to and do hereby relinquish any right or interest that they may have in said notes.

Your petitioners, therefore, pray the Court to enter an order in the said suit, authorizing P. V. Cogbill, substituted trustee, to withdraw the said notes from the papers in said cause, and cancel and mark them paid, and deliver the same to said A. N. Pettigrew, in order that said Pettigrew can have said deed of trust above mentioned, released, or that your Honor will, in some manner, which the Court may deem most judicious andequitable , grant such relief unto your petitioners, as will enable them to release, and your honorable Court to release, the lien of the said deed of trust upon the said property in the said City of Manchester. And your said petitioners pray for such further and general relief as the nature of the case may require, and as to Equity and good conscience may seem meet and just. And your petitioners will ever pray, etc.

Witness C. H. Winfree

Emily X Winfree

W. D. Winfree

Ella Winfree

James W. Winfree

Henry Winfree

J. S. Winfree

Martha Eve Winfree

Witness J. P. Pettigrew

Mariah X Walker

John H. Walker

Lucy J. Hicks

Charles Hicks

Elizabeth X Merrifield

Albert E. Merrifield

NOTES

Chapter 3

1. Weld, *American Slavery as It Is.*
2. Russell, "Free Negro in Virginia."
3. Ibid.
4. Frantel, *Richmond, Virginia Uncovered.*
5. Blackman, *Slavery by Another Name.*
6. Trammel, *Richmond Slave Trade.*
7. Russell, "Free Negro in Virginia."

Chapter 4

8. Clarke, *Narrative of the Sufferings.*
9. Ruggles, *Unboxing of Henry Brown.*
10. Zaborney, *Slaves for Hire.*
11. Ibid.

Chapter 5

12. Weisiger, unpublished research.
13. Ibid.
14. Chesterfield County Historical Society, Winfree files.
15. Goochland County Historical Society, British Camp.
16. Weisiger, *Old Manchester.*

17. Penn University Archives and Records Center, *Selected List of Medical Students.*
18. Family Search, *Virginia Births and Christenings.*
19. Perdue, Barden and Phillips, *Weevils in the Wheat.*
20. National Archives, Jefferson letter.
21. Sublette and Sublette, *American Slave Coast.*

Chapter 6

22. NARA, Compiled Service Records.
23. National Archives, cases examined by the Board of Surgeons.

Chapter 8

24. Campbell, *Richmond's Unhealed History.*
25. Tarter, "Vagrancy Act."
26. Ibid.
27. Nelson, *Steel Drivin' Man: John Henry.*
28. Land Between the Rivers, labor contracts.
29. Valk and Brown, *Living with Jim Crow.*
30. Ibid.
31. Tarter, "First Military District."
32. Alexander, *Race Man.*
33. Ibid.
34. Ibid.
35. Library of Virginia, Warren County List of Colored Applicants Refused Registration.
36. Goldstone, *Inherently Unequal.*
37. Ibid.
38. Trefousse, *Rutherford B. Hayes.*
39. Goldstone, *Inherently Unequal.*
40. Ibid.
41. Wolfe and Baker, "Lynching in Virginia."
42. Feimster, *Southern Horrors.*
43. Alexander, *Race Man.*
44. Wolfe, "Racial Integrity Laws."
45. Wilkerson, *Warmth of Other Suns.*
46. Ibid.
47. Ibid.

Chapter 9

48. Manchester Lodge, *History of Manchester Lodge No. 14.*
49. van Wormer, Jackson and Sudduth, *Maid Narratives.*

BIBLIOGRAPHY

Alexander, Ann Field. *Race Man: The Rise and Fall of the "Fighting Editor" John Mitchell Jr.* Charlottesville: University of Virginia Press, 2002.

Blackman, Douglas A. *Slavery by Another Name.* New York: Anchor Books, 2008.

Blight, David W. *Frederick Douglass: Prophet of Freedom.* New York: Simon and Schuster, 2018.

Campbell, Benjamin. *Richmond's Unhealed History.* Richmond, VA: Brandylane Publishers, 2012.

Chesterfield County Court Records. Emphasis *Upshaw v. Patteson.*

Chesterfield County Historical Society. Winfree vertical files.

Clarke, Lewis. *Narrative of the Sufferings of Lewis Clarke.* Boston: Bela Marsh, 1846, 105–11.

Egerton, Douglas R. *Gabriel's Rebellion.* Chapel Hill: University of North Carolina Press, 1993.

Family Search. Virginia Births and Christenings, 1594–1917.

Feimster, Crystal M. *Southern Horrors: Women and the Politics of Rape and Lynching.* Cambridge, MA: Harvard University Press, 2009.

Frantel, Nancy C. *Richmond, Virginia Uncovered: The Records of Slaves and Free Blacks Listed in the City Sargeant Jail Register, 1841–1846.* Berwyn Heights, MD: Heritage Books, 2010, 16–17.

Goldstone, Lawrence. *Inherently Unequal: The Betrayal of Equal Rights by the Supreme Court, 1865–1903.* N.p., Walker & Company, 2011.

Goochland County Historical Society. British Camp.

The Land Between the Rivers. Piedmont Virginia Digital History, 1866 Labor Contracts for Freedmen Piedmont, Virginia.

Lebsock, Suzanne. *Free Women of Petersburg: Status and Culture in a Southern Town, 1784–1860.* New York: W.W. Norton, 1984.

Library of Virginia. Chesterfield County Chancery Court Records, 1899–1910.

———. Permanent Roll of Voters, Warren County List of Colored Applicants Refused Registration.

———. Petersburg (Va.) Free Negro and Slave Records, 1787–1865.

Manchester Lodge. *History of Manchester Lodge No. 14, A.F. and A.M., 1786–1986.* N.p., 1986, 101.

McGraw, Marie T. *At the Falls: Richmond, Virginia and Its People.* Chapel Hill: University of North Carolina Press, 1994.

National Archives. Founders Online, letter from Thomas Jefferson to Joel Yancy, January 17, 1819.

———. Post Office Manchester, State, Va. (Fold3.com image 9378316). Record of cases examined by the Board of Surgeons in General Hospital at Farmville, Va. December 23, 1864.

National Archives and Records Administration (NARA). Compiled Service Records of Confederate Soldiers Who Served in Organizations from the State of Virginia, NAI, Series Number M324, Roll 363. Washington, D.C.

Nelson, Scott Reynolds. *Steel Drivin' Man: John Henry: The Untold Story of an American Legend.* Oxford, UK: Oxford University Press, 2006.

Penn University Archives and Records Center. Selected List of Medical Students 1805–1860. Catalog of the trustees, officers and medical class 1837–1838, Philadelphia.

Perdue, Charles L., Jr., Thomas E. Barden, and Robert K. Phillips, eds. *Weevils in the Wheat: Interviews with Virginia Ex-Slaves.* Charlottesville: University Press of Virginia, 1976, 291.

Petersburg Courthouse Records. Inventory of Estate of Jordan Branch, Petersburg Will Book #44, 445.

Ruggles, Jeffrey. *The Unboxing of Henry Brown.* Richmond: Library of Virginia, 2003.

Russell, John Henderson. "The Free Negro in Virginia, 1619–1865." Ph.D. diss., Johns Hopkins, 1913, 112–16.

Stevens, Charles E. *Anthony Burns: A History.* N.p.: Corner House, 1973.

Sublette, Ned, and Constance Sublette. *The American Slave Coast: A History of the Slave Breeding Industry.* New York: Lawrence Hill Books, 2016, 353–58.

Tarter, Brent. "First Military District." Encyclopedia of Virginia, Virginia Humanities, August 27, 2015.

————. "Vagrancy Act of 1866." Encyclopedia of Virginia, Virginia Humanities, August 25, 2015.

Trammel, Jack. *The Richmond Slave Trade: The Economic Backbone of the Old Dominion*. Charleston, SC: The History Press, 2012.

Trefousse, Hans L. *Rutherford B. Hayes*. New York: Henry Holt and Co., 2002.

Valk, Anne, and Leslie Brown. *Living with Jim Crow: African American Women and Memories of the Segregated South*. New York: Palgrave McMillan, 2010.

van Wormer, Katherine, David W. Jackson III and Charletta Sudduth. *The Maid Narratives: Black Domestics and White Families in the Jim Crow South*. Baton Rouge: Louisiana State University Press, 2012.

Virginia Museum of History and Culture. Record Book of Branch and Son, Petersburg, 1858.

————. Records of Manchester Lodge #14.

Weisiger, Benjamin B., III. *Old Manchester and Its Environs, 1769–1910*. Richmond, VA: William Byrd Press, 1993.

————. Unpublished research, with permission from Minor Weisiger.

Weld, Theodore Dwight. *American Slavery as It Is: Testimony of a Thousand Witnesses*. N.p.: American Slavery Society, 1838, 85.

Wilkerson, Isabel. *The Warmth of Other Suns*. New York: Vintage Books, 2010.

Wolfe, Brendan. "Racial Integrity Laws (1924–1930)." Encyclopedia of Virginia, 2021.

Wolfe, Brendan, and Laura K. Baker. "Lynching in Virginia." Encyclopedia of Virginia, Virginia Humanities, June 4, 2020.

Zaborney, John J. *Slaves for Hire: Renting Enslaved Laborers in Antebellum Virginia*. Baton Rouge: Louisiana State University Press, 2012.

INDEX

ABOUT THE AUTHORS

*D*r. Jan Meck (*left*) and Virginia Refo (*right*) are both native Virginians and long-term residents of Richmond. Dr. Meck is a retired NASA scientist, and Virginia Refo is a retired foster care and adoption social worker and an experienced genealogist. Since retirement, they have been docents and researchers at the Virginia Museum of History and Culture and received the Volunteers of the Year Award in 2019 for their work on this book. Dr. Meck also gives a free tour titled "African American Heroes of Richmond." They have been working together since November 2017, gathering information from courthouses, libraries, historical societies, community organizations and Emily Winfree's descendants.

Visit us at
www.historypress.com